WHOM
THE
LORD
LOVETH

My son, despise not the chastening of the Lord,
nor faint when thou art rebuked of him:
For whom the Lord loveth he chasteneth,
and scourgeth every son whom he receiveth.

—Paul's Epistle to the Hebrews.

WHOM
THE
LORD
LOVETH

THE STORY OF JAMES A. HUFF

JANE HUFF

McGRAW-HILL BOOK COMPANY, INC.

New York   Toronto   London

Library of Congress Catalog Card Number: 61-7579

First Edition

30858

Foreword

*"Now faith is the assurance of things hoped for,
the conviction of things not seen."*

Through the centuries of man's history, there has always been
a small minority who walked by faith, almost always a little
strange to their times, their faces alight with the vision of a
distant Kingdom, though they themselves live and move in
the realities of the human predicament.

They seem to experience life in deeper measure, to an extra
dimension; they reach a rare depth and fullness which is difficult to explain outside the faith which guides and sustains
them. They may sometimes be storm tossed and troubled . . .
yet their decisions are not made by the expediency of this
world, but by the standards of the next. Perhaps the only thing
common to all of them is the open heart, the questing spirit,
which leads them out of the ordinary paths of life to the full
venture of faith.

It is of such a man that I must write. Unfortunately, those
of us who have the time to write biographies never have the
stature and vision of the men whose stories we write. Our
viewpoint must necessarily be limited. Nevertheless, I must
tell what I can, though I find the writing difficult. Where
do you begin to pick up the tangled threads which make up
the story of a life? What do you tell, and what do you leave
untold? I can only begin with what I saw, and add where I
can what others have told me. . . .

I feel I am more of an editor than a writer, I have borrowed so freely from the thoughts of others. Through friendship, study, love, and faith, my own life has been so rich in experiences of mind and spirit, I cannot begin to acknowledge my debt to others, So many people have shaped my thinking and thus contributed to the writing of this book: my mother, whose gift of words and love of the English language gave me the tools for writing; Helen and George Hoffman Smith, who opened the door to a lifetime adventure in the Christian faith; to all those of the Huff and Wilson "clan" who bore with me and taught me more than I realized at the time; and to that great body of ministers and teachers who have tried to illumine the Word of God for me and others like me.

It is impossible to separate and acknowledge my indebtedness—or to repay it—I can only set down what I have seen and learned, so those who follow after me may know that God is actively at work in the hearts and lives of men today; that to those who live by faith, Christ is the victory which overcomes the world.

Jane Huff

WHOM
THE
LORD
LOVETH

BOOK I

THE VISION

*"Where there is no vision,
the people perish."*

PROVERBS 29:18

Chapter 1

IT WAS NOT an auspicious beginning. I was cross and embarrassed, impatient and, worst of all, late.

I hate to be late. I hate to be late anywhere, but especially when I'm among strangers. I am deaf; if I am to hear anything at all I must sit in front. A smaller person might slip down front inconspicuously, but I am so tall I am *never* inconspicuous. I've always minded that I tower over most people; it is agony to walk late into a group I don't know, and parade down to the front as if I were careless or thoughtless or unconcerned.

But this time there was no help for it. It had been difficult to persuade my mother that it was perfectly safe for my sister Martha and me to drive thirty miles alone in broad daylight, from Jacksonville Beach to the Presbyterian church in St. Augustine, for a conference of Christian Endeavor leaders. I was almost twenty, and with the impatience of youth I was thoroughly annoyed that she should hesitate so long about letting us use the car. So we got off to a late start. I had promised not to speed, and kept my word, though I fumed all the way down to St. Augustine.

By the time we found a parking place and got into the church, the sound of singing inside warned us that the worship service had begun. As we approached the sanctuary there was a silence, evidently for a prayer, then the piano began again. I was squirming inside. I could see a good-sized crowd in the back of the church, a few empty seats at the front. I hated to walk down in front of everyone—but it would be stupid to sit in back and not hear anything.

I put my chin up and whispered to Martha, "Come on, we'll go sit in front." I marched down the aisle before she could object. She was a quarter of an inch taller than I—and could hear a pin drop in the next room. But I was a year older, so she meekly followed elder sister down the aisle.

I had a confused notion of several people in the front of the church—but the one who stood out was the song leader. He was young, with cottony blond hair and a candid, almost boyish, face. His eyes had an infectious gaiety, and I noticed they followed us all the way down the aisle even while he was leading the hymn. I also noticed, with the sure instinct of every girl cursed with surplus inches, that he was taller than I.

Just as I was beginning to hope that the floor would open beneath us, Martha and I found seats. Someone handed us a songbook, and as I took the book and began to sing, the song leader caught my eye and smiled—a glad, warm, "Hello-we're-so-glad-you-came" sort of smile. Somehow, this silent greeting made us a part of the group. It didn't matter anymore that we were late or that I had to sit down front. His welcome kept us from being strangers. The flush left my cheeks and I relaxed.

That song ended the worship service. The man nearest Martha turned to her and said, "Hi! I'm Bob Sherrod from Tennessee. Where did you girls come from?"

We introduced ourselves and were quickly greeted by others: "We're glad you came. I'm Betty McKnight, from Richmond." "W. D. Smith from Alabama," in a rich drawl. ... "Carroll Wright from Boston...." We were then sent off to separate conferences, and the morning was quickly gone.

We had promised Mother to return her car as soon as the morning session was over. Martha and I decided to buy some books before we left. We were gathering our purchases when the song leader came up to us. (Our programs had identified him as James A. Huff from Tennessee.) "Hi, Jane," he said, "You're not leaving now, are you?"

I was surprised. How had he learned my name? I hadn't seen him again during the morning and hadn't realized he had given me much notice. He had the look of a man whose life overflowed with humor and kindness, and his smile at me earlier had been no more than a welcome, an assurance that we had not really interrupted the service.

I looked up at him. "Yes," I explained slowly, "we promised Mother we would return her car."

"Don't go," he said urgently. "You'll miss the fun. We're all eating lunch together and then going for a swim. Phone home to ask if you can stay. Some of us can drive you home after the evening service," he added thoughtfully, "so tell your folks you won't be driving alone."

Taking our courage in hand, we phoned Mother collect. Dad did not approve of collect calls and it wasn't likely he'd approve of our staying late. But such was Jim Huff's assurance we *would* phone, and *could* stay, that we tried it, and received Mother's permission to stay until after the evening meeting, provided that we were escorted home. As Martha hung up the phone, we looked at each other, quite amazed at our success. Jim Huff had certainly inspired us with his enthusiasm.

We left the church office and found Bob Sherrod waiting for us. "Jim went out to take movies of the crowd," he said. "You two come on out." Bob winked at us. "We call him Pathé News. He has a certain liking for cameras. . . ."

It was an understatement. As we walked out of the dim, vine-covered old church into the brilliant July sunlight, Jim was standing at the foot of the steps taking movies. Around his neck was slung another camera, a light meter, and a canvas bag of photographic gear. "Don't you girls get away," he called. "I want to take some stills, then we'll go to lunch. I'll find someone to lend you bathing suits so you can swim this afternoon." Evidently he didn't leave anything to chance.

As good as his word, after lunch he found a friend to loan us suits. To my surprise, Martha and I were the only girls in the crowd who honestly could swim. Most of the others had been raised inland, but we had grown up beside the water and it seemed that I could swim better than I could do anything else. The tide was coming in and the waves were high and exhilarating. Jim and I were still diving through the waves when the others had quit; then we went in to play ball on the beach. Jim in his exuberance was at the center of everything.

We had supper with the crowd, then Jim served as song leader for the short evening conference. When it was over, he asked Bob to drive my sister home in our car and volunteered to drive me in his. I was beginning to take it for granted that people were drawn to Jim wherever he went, and we soon collected quite a group.

Obviously Cotton, as his friends called him, was a joyous, friendly, exuberant person—a leader of men. He had poise and charm—though I did wonder if he might not be just a bit spoiled by his good fortune, for his profuse photographic equipment and robin's-egg-blue convertible gave evidence of rather more wealth than is usually possessed by the average person at a Christian Endeavor convention.

Yet, I knew he couldn't have been a leader of that meeting if he were not talented and willing to use his talents in God's service. I definitely liked him and wanted to know him better. We rode north along the ocean, singing as we went. I sat next to Cotton on the front seat; and under cover of the songs, we talked, each seeking the words to unlock the personality of the other, drawn to each other, yet each a little wary of revealing too much interest or too much of ourselves.

Everyone my age was interested in the new draft law which was then being debated in Congress.

"How will it affect you?" I asked him.

I had seen during the afternoon that he was a natural athlete; he excelled at everything we had done. His answer surprised me. "Oh, I'm afraid it won't touch me at all. I'm thirty-three, and I guess it will reach the younger fellows first. Besides, I'm diabetic, so I'll probably have to stick to my activities in the National Guard."

I was surprised at his age—he looked so much younger. And at the time, I had only the faintest notion what diabetes was. He looked too rugged and big and healthy for me to imagine that it really mattered.

The ride home was over too soon. Jim came in to meet my mother and father and persuaded them to let us go to St. Augustine again the following day for another session of the conference.

When he had gone, I went to my room. It had been an exciting day. There was little enough to go on—but I was young and awkward and shy, and someone special had singled me out of a crowd. I undressed and crawled into bed and lay there, wide awake, going over the events of the day. . . .

Why does the heart choose one and only one in a crowd? What had made this man stand out for me? Was it the warmth of his smile in the early morning which had made me feel less a stranger, more a part of the group? Was it the interests we shared and the circumstances in which we met? Was it the lovely, warm, rich voice which caught at the heart—and made a special appeal to me, who could not carry a tune? Was it the gaiety, the assurance, that particular quality of leadership which had all of us following after him?

I couldn't have answered then, and I can't really answer today. But for me, the man had a charm beyond fathoming. That night I went to bed warm and content to have met him, to dream and hope as only the young can dream and hope. When you are young, life seems a fairy tale, and love can have but one ending.

But life is not a fairy tale; life's heroes and heroines are more complex, and the obvious and expected does not always happen.

Not that I was disappointed, at first. In less than a week a letter came from Jim. It was gay: "Hi, remember me? I'm that fellow you met in St. Augustine . . ." and it ended, "Love, Jim." My frivolous, foolish heart pounced on the word. But I tried to admonish myself: "That doesn't mean anything. All Southerners sign everything, 'Love.' It's just a word."

Of course, though, to me it was more than a word. It was a whisper of hope, food for dreams. I answered his letter—and all the chain of letters that followed.

Fall and winter slipped away, and our early Florida spring swelled and ripened. The gardenias were more profuse and luxuriant than I had ever seen them, filling the air with their rich beauty and fragrance. I gathered them in wide flat baskets and floated masses of the translucent white blossoms in shallow crystal bowls. I kept them on my desk at the office, on the coffee table in the living room at home, and in my bedroom— the opulent scent was everywhere. It, too, was food for dreams, as were Cotton's letters which were now urging me to come to Tennessee.

"Come in May," he wrote. "We'll go to Wonderland Park above Gatlinburg for the Smoky Mountains District Christian Endeavor convention. You'll see some of the folks you met last summer in St. Augustine, as well as lots more wonderful people. You may even meet a few eligible bachelors. . . ."

The casual tone bothered me. I wanted to go—but I didn't want to seem too eager. There was reason for going. I was slated for the presidency of our district Christian Endeavor union and could learn a good deal from the meeting—but for me, the only *real* reason was to see Jim and meet his family. . . .

He wrote several more times—and I went. Two days before

I was to go, I had a bad fall and cracked a pair of ribs. The doctor plastered my sides with layers of adhesive tape and told me to be quiet for a few days—so I went quietly to Tennessee. It would have taken more than broken ribs to keep me away by then. After I arrived, even the pain couldn't diminish the excitement of that meeting.

The year before in St. Augustine, Jim had stood out as someone special; but in his own home territory he had the aura of a crown prince, one who was particularly wise and beloved, possessed of a humor and charm which made a delightful adventure of commonplace happenings. Yet he also possessed a touch of humility which made people somehow identify themselves with him. And too, his charm went deeper, growing out of the essential selflessness of the man. Never had I met anyone who gave so freely of himself to others, and behind this giving lay a spiritual depth and purpose which went far beyond the mere desire to please. He loved his fellow men so much that they could hardly help but love him back. At any rate, I knew then that I loved him.

Jim met me in Gatlinburg and drove me up to the old hotel —a remnant of the great frame "gingerbread" resort hotels of another era. From the moment we arrived, he was the center of attention: "Jim, the dining room wants to change the meal schedule. Will it be all right?" "Six people came from Knoxville who hadn't registered—we're already overflowing, should we take them?" (Jim's answer, "Sure, they can sleep on the floor if there's no place else. . . .") It was an inspiring gathering—and a revealing one, for what it showed of Jim. But in one way it was deeply dispiriting. Everyone seemed to take it for granted that I was "Jim's girl," but he himself made no particular effort to single me out or to be with me.

There are a few people with whom I feel a deep kinship, and about whose thoughts and feelings I have that sharply intuitive sense which sometimes sees into the heart. As Jim now became withdrawn—though it would scarcely have been apparent to anyone but me—I could almost read his thoughts. He hadn't remained a bachelor without having a real determination not to be "trapped"—and however attractive I might seem to him, he just had no intention of marrying and didn't want me to have any false hopes.

I guessed he had formed some deep reservation about marriage. What it was, I didn't know—nor could I ask. Yet I wondered. Was it that monastic streak which runs in some few men? Was it just a wariness of marriage itself? Perhaps he was just so beloved and so surrounded by people that he felt unwilling or unable to concentrate his love on one person alone. Whatever it was, it remained unspoken, but it caused a constraint between us which made a disappointment of the brief visit to his home.

Once I returned home again, the tension between us seemed gone. "Writing letters to you is really fun," he wrote. "I've been reading back over some of those you've written me, and we must really have exchanged some high-class ideas."

The letters *were* fun, and I loved them—but I also knew I was perilously close to loving the man more than I should. I tried more than once to stop writing him, lest I lose control of my feelings—but always he wrote back some particularly appealing letter. Our deep interest in religion formed a strong bond between us. By now I was president of my district Christian Endeavor union, and he was vice-president of the International Christian Endeavor union, with the nine Southern states as his particular field. We wrote continually of the work to be done.

I attempted to put an end to our correspondence. His reply, "I need you to be always jogging me to get something done. No one else does this for me . . ." was more than I could turn down. I continued to "jog" him with ideas, asking if he had finished this project or that. When our program chairman invited him to be the speaker at our first big meeting in the fall, he wrote, "Your letter of the twelfth is certainly a welcome sight. I thought I was on your black list for good. It has been so long since I heard from you. I would like to come to Florida, not only for the meeting, but just to see you. . . . Keep writing and sending in ideas for this Southern work. You kind of keep me going, which is what I need. Love, Jim."

My hopes rose again. Apparently he realized it. He took time to be alone with me, and here he tried to tell me why he couldn't marry.

He had idly picked up a twig as we walked down to the water's edge after one of the sessions. Now he broke it bit by bit and threw each piece into the lake, in the deliberately off-hand manner of one who has an unpleasant duty to perform. . . . He did not look at me at all, but with his eyes intently followed each bit of flotsam as it arched through the air and landed in the water. His voice was casual, almost disinterested, as he began, "You know, I'll probably never marry. I guess it'll take me the rest of my life to earn enough to live in the manner to which I'd like to become accustomed. . . ."

I guess my mouth fell open as I thought, "Ha! I'll bet *you* never have to worry about money. . . ." He was at that time general manager of a hosiery-manufacturing company employing seven hundred people. My feminine pride could bear no more. I couldn't even hear him out.

"Think no more of it, friend," I reassured him crisply. "I've never chased a man yet, and I have no intention of proposing to one, so you're quite safe. If ever you want anything more than friendship, you're going to have to come to me."

He looked more than startled for a moment as he turned to face me, then his hearty laughter rang out. "If ever I do want more, Miss Jane," he said with a mock formality which quite became him, "I'll come to you."

As a sudden thundershower clears the air and leaves behind it an atmosphere that is sharp and clean and sweet, so this little exchange cleared the air of our relationship. Now I could be light and easy with him, and he could be relaxed with me.

So light and easy did our relationship remain, that, by the time I was twenty-four, I was sure I was going to live up to my father's dire prediction that I was bound to be an old maid. I had broken off with my other beaux, one by one—my crowd was scattered around the world in the various services.

And then, not long before Christmas, Jim wrote to ask if he could come to Florida to see me during the holidays. Of course, I would enjoy seeing him again. There was always a lift in his presence, a contagious joy about him. If I had any more romantic expectations, I put them out of my mind. I wrote back at once that I wanted him to come.

Jim had Christmas with his family, then came down the following day on the train, arriving in time for lunch. After we had eaten, we wandered into the garden. A mild winter had blessed us with poinsettias; the beautiful camellias were in bloom everywhere, their exquisite soft pastel blossoms in sharp contrast to the dark glossy leaves.

We walked out to benches by the brook, and as we seated ourselves in the thin wintry sunlight, Jim looked at me wryly and said, "Well, you said you always knew what I was thinking. . . ." He paused, almost as if waiting for *me* to finish!

"Oh, no," I thought in vehement protest. "All the years I've wished for this proposal and envisaged a tender romantic scene. I won't, I *won't* have it this way." Aloud, I said, "Well, if it's what I think it is, I don't want to hear it in my own back yard, in broad daylight, within sound and sight of all the neighbors! I've known you for four and one-half years, and you've only asked me for *two dates*. If you have anything to say to me, you can say it properly." I was so angry, I was sputtering.

Jim's face lighted up in a grin, and he looked especially gleeful. He stood, very formally, stretched up to his full six feet two inches, and bowed from the waist. "Miss Coughlan," he said in his most proper tone, "will you do me the honor of dining and dancing with me this evening?"

I rose to my six feet one-half inch (I was wearing shoes),

curtsied with equal formality. "Mr. Huff, I would be delighted." He gave me his arm, and we returned to the house together.

Dinner was gay and informal, in a quiet place. Later, we drove across the river to a bluff where we could look back and see the lights of Jacksonville across the water. We sat quietly for a minute, then he gently took my hand—he had that oddly comforting streak of gentleness often found in strong, vital men—and began purposefully.

"Jane, you told me I would have to come to you to propose. Will you marry me?"

Long and eagerly as I had awaited the question, it had an odd effect on me. I was somehow shocked into uncertainty.

"Oh, Jim, I don't know, I don't know. You've never even kissed me," I said, irrationally.

Then he kissed me as thoroughly as he should have done four years earlier. For the first time I was sure that he was in love with me, that he hadn't just decided to get married and chosen me as the most suitable candidate! Yet the uncertainty his proposal had roused remained. I could not, I felt, promise to marry him without taking more time to think. "Take whatever time you need," Jim told me.

For the two remaining days of his visit, he did not refer again to his proposal, but played the role of hopeful suitor— an utterly delightful role, and one new to him. He did it with gaiety, gallantry, and a complete aplomb that he had in any situation. I wished he could have stayed longer, but wartime was no time for long vacations for businessmen.

When it was time for Jim to go, I still had not given him an answer. The decision was not easy one. I had been so ready to love him with all my heart in the first year I knew him; now that "first, fine rapture" was gone. The years of being so cautious, of being so sure he would never marry, of trying never to think of him as more than a friend, had had their insidious effect.

Although I wanted to decide with my heart, maturity made me ask questions before I committed myself. I wondered about living in Rockwood. I had visited there twice in the years I had known Jim, and there was a quality about it that awed me— there was so very much family. It might be quite difficult indeed.

Another question was the difference in ages. My father had been much older than Mother—and he had died just a year before, leaving Mother a widow at forty-three. This made the difference between Jim's age and mine seem so much more important. How long would I be left alone? Jim tried to answer this one, saying that his father was seventy and his mother in her sixties, so I ought to be sure of twenty-five years of married life. Later the memory of this prediction would return, with poignant meaning.

Then there was Jim's boundless energy. We shared a deep commitment to God and both loved our church work. But Jim's selfless interest in other people, his eagerness to communicate his own joy in religion kept him constantly in action. The pace frightened me, and I wondered whether I would ever have the greatness of soul to follow him.

These were the questions. But it *is* the heart which finally decides. I had been willing to love Jim from the beginning, but simply hadn't dared love him too much. Now at last, freed from the long restraint, that love began to grow as a plant thrives in the sun. When Jim had left my home that Christmastime, I had still feared to give him my promise. But within days of his departure I knew that this was the man for me.

Chapter 2

Happy is the bride the sun shines upon." Our wedding day in June dawned cool and fair. We were to be married in Atlanta—partly because it was a more convenient meeting ground for our extensive families than my mother's Florida home, but also because it was close to where I then had a job. How swiftly the months had passed by! Ours could hardly have been described as a whirlwind courtship, yet Jim grew ever more impatient for us to be married. Now, after six months which had gone by as swiftly as six days, I was to start a whole new life.

The last few days had been hectic, though spiced with anticipation. I longed for a little time to myself to sit down and think, to collect myself and relax. Since Mother and Martha were staying some distance away, I had decided to dress alone at the church. I looked forward to this brief period of solitude, when I could indulge in the luxury of dressing slowly—and engage in a little quiet meditation.

At the store where I had bought my wedding dress, the bridal consultant had sternly warned me, "Now, don't open the box or take the gown out until you're ready to put it on! It will be packed so there won't be a wrinkle in it when you open it—but if you try it on ahead of time we can't be responsible."

In the dressing room at the church I spread out a sheet to

15

protect the dress, then opened the box. Is there anything like the texture of a white satin wedding gown? This was luscious and heavy, simply and beautifully cut, with no ornament. I reveled in the liquid, pearly look of it.

Alas, the gown had *not* been properly packed. Although it was wrapped in multitudinous layers of tissue, these hadn't kept the dress and train from wrinkling. From the crumpled look of it, they might as well have sent it jammed into a laundry bag!

"Oh, vanity, vanity." My heart sank as I spread out the dress and train—no eye could possibly escape seeing how disheveled it was. There was less than an hour until the wedding ceremony was to begin, and it was clearly too late to call the store. If anything were to be done, I would have to do it myself.

The church is a very present help in spiritual troubles; I now hoped it would assist in more worldly ways. I went quickly to the office, found the church secretary, and told her my plight. For a minute, she couldn't suggest anything. Then she said, "My apartment isn't far away. If you'll stay here and answer the telephone, I'll go home and get an iron." Off she went.

The minutes crept by. Gone was the spirit of calm and peace for which I had hoped. It was probably no more than ten minutes before she returned, but I had miserable visions of Jim waiting at the altar while I ironed my dress.

"Here," said my good Samaritan, as she came breathlessly through the door. "I think you still have forty minutes."

We had no ironing board, so she sat on the couch and held a fourteen-inch-square cushion on her lap while I nervously pressed the gown over it. The train seemed to grow in size as I ironed square after square after square. We were both almost hysterical by the time I finished. But I had slipped on the dress and was buttoning the last button when Mother and Martha came in.

"The traffic was so heavy," said Mother, more than a little

flustered, "it took us twenty minutes longer to come back than we thought. The organ has already begun to play." I had been so engrossed in getting ready that I had not even realized they were late. Mother leaned over to kiss me before she left, taking both my hands in hers. "Darling, I wish you all the happiness that marriage can bring," she said and went out to take her seat in the chapel.

Martha lingered to help me put on my veil and wished me luck as we moved out to take our places for the ceremony. I know I looked calm—I usually *look* calm no matter how I feel—but I was churning inside. In place of the minutes of meditation and prayer I had planned, I now found myself muttering in a way that might have seemed blasphemous, "God, *why* do I always start everything on my left foot?"

Martha had started sedately down the aisle, and I, lost in a silent colloquy with God, followed almost on her heels when I was suddenly jerked back into the present. My brother, who had come to give me away, caught my arm to warn me I had started before my cue. In his urgency his powerful hand almost crushed my arm—but it served effectively to bring me back to earth.

Jim, walking across the front of the chapel to his place, caught my eye, and revealed by the merest flicker of an eyelid that he had seen me enter too soon. His warm, sweet expression didn't change at all, but I knew if we were alone, he would have raised one eyebrow and asked, "Eager?"

I turned crimson with embarrassment and couldn't bear to look at him for a moment. Then I realized it was right to be eager! As I looked again at his merry face, I saw he was just as eager, just as glad as I.

"My cup runneth over," I thought, for I felt as if I were bursting with happiness at the promise of the life ahead of us. I came down the aisle to my appointed place. Dr. Orr, Jim's beloved minister, had come from Rockwood to marry us. Resembling a benevolent, elderly cherub in a morning coat, he

began the marriage service: "Dearly beloved, we are assembled here in the presence of God. . . ." The words were familiar, but newly charged with personal meaning as we each
pledged our troth to the other. Dr. Orr placed my hand in
Jim's, saying the words which Jim, with glowing face, repeated
after him: "I, James, take thee, Jane, to be my wedded wife,
and I do promise and covenant, before God and these wit-
nesses, to be thy loving and faithful husband, in plenty and in
want, in joy and in sorrow, in sickness and in health, as long
as we both shall live."

Then I, in my turn, made the same pledge. With that odd
mixture of high idealism and honest realism with which we
both approached life, we made our promises—but I am sure
neither of us had any real idea how much these promises were
to require of each of us. Even if we had known, neither of us
would have made any move to turn back.

We knelt to receive the benediction, and it was over. Jim
saluted me with a kiss, then tucking my arm in his started out
of the church at such a breathless pace, he was almost running.
I hung on and ran with him. In fact, ever afterward I ran to
keep up with him.

The man whose life I had promised to share was still very
much a stranger. I loved him deeply, but he had many qualities
which I still did not understand, many, I must admit, which
frightened me a little.

I was overwhelmed by his enormous vitality, a seemingly
insatiable appetite for life. I feared I simply could never keep
up with him. More important, my woman's intuition sensed
deep within him a powerful restlessness, a spiritual discontent
which he kept secret from the world and from me. What it was
I did not know. Surely here was a man who had everything
anyone might wish to make him happy. What more could he
want? I felt uneasy and inadequate in the presence of this
hidden side of Jim; in the way of a woman, I wanted to be
everything to him, yet I knew in my heart I could not.

His inner restlessness often showed itself in a sort of prank-ishness and unconventionality which usually delighted but sometimes rather unnerved me. I got my first good taste of it on our way home from our honeymoon.

The sun was shining and Jim seemed to radiate enthusiasm. He was so very exuberant that I was quite touched, thinking, naturally, that his joy sprang from the fact that he was on his honeymoon, and it was just a time to be happy.

I rode happily beside him in the hot June sunshine. From the open car I watched mile after mile of corn and the cotton fields on either hand. The dreamy monotony of the passing countryside made me drowsy.

Suddenly, though, I was wide awake. It had slowly pene-trated my consciousness that the last road signs had indicated that home lay in the opposite direction. "Jim," I asked, "aren't we going the wrong way?"

"Nope," he answered gaily.

"Where are we going?"

"You'll see."

Passing a large military airfield, he abruptly swung left into what was evidently a storage area. Here were lined up, row after row, airplanes and gliders.

"Well, here we are."

I was completely mystified but got out and followed him. He seemed to have his mind set on seeing a particular kind of glider, but he couldn't find it. Someone came over to help him —and before I had quite realized what was going on, we were the proud (on his part) and astonished (on mine) owners of a two-passenger glider, complete with its own trailer.

I was too newly married to open my mouth before a stranger. By the time the trailer had been fastened to the back of the car and we were driving away, I was bursting.

"Cotton, what on *earth* are you going to do with a glider?"

"Why, we'll fly it."

"But neither of us can fly!"

"No, *I* can't get a license because I'm diabetic. But if *you* get one, then I can fly any time I'm in the plane with you. I thought later we might even get a small plane," he went on blithely. "It would save worlds of time on business trips, and you could just go everywhere with me."

"Jim, Jim," I laughed helplessly, "you're crazy!"

"That's right," he agreed good humoredly. "It's a sad case: When the Lord saw what He had done, He broke the mold and threw away the pieces so it wouldn't happen again."

He soon found he couldn't drive at any speed with the trailer for it bucked and swayed in the wind created by the car. He had to slow to a very sedate pace to allow it a calm passage. The glider was an ungainly thing about three times as long as the car. With its wings folded back against its body, and encased in a tightly fitting canvas cover, it looked for all the world like a giant dragonfly struggling to emerge from its chrysalis. As we passed through little towns on our way, heads swiveled around at us, and people gesticulated excitedly.

I must have fallen asleep shortly after we crossed the Tennessee River in Chattanooga. We drove through the tunnel and turned into the valley which extends for more than seventy miles northward. Walden's Ridge, the eastern outpost of the Cumberland Plateau, rose abruptly on our left; the Tennessee River lay ever hidden from view by lesser hills to the east.

We were nearing Spring City when Jim called, "Jane, Jane, wake up. There's the smoke of Rockwood up the valley—the first sign of home!"

I woke with a start and looked around. The sun had dropped below the mountains on our left. The light that remained had a special, luminous quality, and everything stood out with great clarity. On our left, neatly divided north and south by the railroad, were rich green meadows where cattle grazed. In the far distance, where the mountains on our left and the hills on our right merged at the skyline, one great plume of smoke made an exclamation point over the valley.

We reached Rockwood at an inopportune time, for we drove up Kingston Avenue just as the two Methodist churches ended evening services. One church was right on the avenue, the other a block away. The dispersing crowds were meeting at the stop light, which turned red as we approached. We and our peculiar appendage were halted under the street lights, right in the midde of a curious crowd.

I cannot remember a word of what was said. Everybody seemed to know instinctively who it was. The amused comments from Jim's swarm of friends embarrassed me, but Jim took it all in good part. He was used to being kidded about everything he did, and sat there, to use his own phrase, "as happy as if he had good sense," until the light changed. Then we drove down the last block to the apartment which was our first home.

The white frame Victorian house before which we stopped had, in a day of large families and many servants, been a single-family home. It had lately been divided into four pleasant apartments with big, high-ceilinged, large-windowed rooms of another era.

Jim carried our bags into the hall. Setting them down, he triumphantly produced a key, then flinging open the door, he turned, scooped me up in his arms, and carried me over the threshold so easily that it made six-foot me feel small and dainty.

"Oh, Jim," I laughed, caught by surprise, "what a nice romantic gesture!"

"Well, I promised you twenty-five years of romance," he said as he kissed me and set me down. "We might as well begin it properly." He added a phrase that was to become a ritual for all the homecomings afterward, "Welcome home, Mrs. Huff. I'm mighty glad to have you here."

"I'm so glad to be here, love," I replied.

And I *was* glad. As I looked up into his face and saw the joy and delight, and the very real pride that was written there,

I wanted at the same time to thank him for being so gallant and to pledge anew my love for him, which at this moment was overwhelming.

Jim's hands tightened on my shoulders, his expression became more serious, and he bowed his head to include God in this moment of homecoming and dedication: "Lord, we thank you for a safe journey home, for the love we have for one another, and for the love of Christ which has given us so much. Bless us as we begin this home together, and keep us from being selfish—use us, we pray, in Your service. Help us to share our love of Christ with others. These things we ask in His name and for His sake. Amen."

He looked at me seriously for a long moment. Then he said lightly, "Well, I can't leave those bags out all night." And he went to fetch them.

Chapter 3

THERE ARE many poor jokes made about what happens when the honeymoon is over. Yet there is a grain of truth in all the cynical humor about the stresses and strains which pull at a marriage after the first flush of romance. I knew all this—and I knew also that our love for each other was strong enough to withstand any strain. But while I felt I could face any major troubles that might develop, I was not really prepared to handle the trivial problems of everyday living that did come.

In the first months of our marriage, I had much to learn. I had to learn not only to adjust my life to Jim's, but also to live comfortably with his large family in his small home town. This was the hardest.

I have long since learned to love small towns, as I have grown to know them—and myself—better, but then it was new and difficult for me. There are times and places when I feel poised and sure, confident I can cope in the give-and-take of life. At other times and other places my poise deserts me; I become dumb and awkward, and so very unsure.

Often, all too often, this was the way I felt during my first months at Rockwood, for I could not escape the feeling that I was being watched, watched all the time. Every action acquired a distorted importance.

This, I think, is one of the most characteristic features of small-town living—and especially of Southern small towns. There watching, just watching, is a universal occupation. William Polk describes it most delightfully in his book *Southern Accent*. "The first and great commandment," he says, "is, 'Know thy neighbor as thyself.' The pursuit of this knowledge is a fine art, an exact science, the chief amusement and the most popular indoor and outdoor sport of the region. Everything about each resident and the stranger within his gates is seen, noted, discussed, and disseminated—*everything*—including his ancestors, his family, his acts, his tastes, habits, faith, idiosyncrasies, emotions and motives, how long he says his prayers and wears his socks, what woman he cocked an eye at in church on Sunday."

I recall vividly an early brush with small-town customs. It was on a day when we were going on a picnic, and I was dressed for it. Since I had been raised in Florida, I had worn shorts all my life, fairly short shorts at that. That morning I had unconcernedly put on smart black shorts with a trim yellow shirt I had made for my trousseau. I was especially fond of this outfit because Jim always whistled when I wore it.

I packed lunch and suddenly realized I had no mustard. I put everything in the car and planned to go to the grocery store before picking up Jim at his office.

Luckily, there was a parking place in front of the barbershop next to the grocery. I pulled in and hopped out of the car. An overalled farmer was just coming out of the barbershop. He glanced in my direction, gulped, and backed into the barber's. Intent on my errand, I wasn't really aware of him until I realized that there were three farmers coming out and two barbers at the window, ALL LOOKING AT ME!!! These men didn't whistle, they just *looked*. I turned crimson and fled to the car.

When I got to Jim's office, he was waiting for me. "Jane," he said, "I just had a phone call." He paused, then grinned, "You know, now that I think of it, *I've* never seen a woman in shorts on the streets of Rockwood either!"

We drove back to the store and parked on the opposite side of the street. I sat in the car while *he* got the mustard.

In my self-consciousness it seemed to me I was always running afoul of other people's feelings. I received an invitation to join a sewing club which met weekly—on the same day as a small bridge group to which I had been invited several times. I've always wished I had been born with the gift of diplomacy, for I've never really been able to cultivate it.

Furthermore, the invitation had come over the telephone, where I am always at my worst: Even when I can hear perfectly well, I am conditioned by years of deafness and frequent misunderstandings, so I am always uncomfortable unless the conversation is with a friend who knows me well enough to discount any strange replies.

Yet even I was a little awed to hear myself saying, all *too* frankly, "Thank you so much. I'd love to come and be with you occasionally, but I really don't want to sew a whole afternoon every single week. I'd much rather play bridge than sew."

Of course, by the time I had heard what I had said, it was too late to take it back. I tried to smooth it over, but there really wasn't any graceful way out. My face was burning, and I held the telephone hoping it didn't sound quite so dreadful as I feared.

Foolish hope. Before the day was over, my long-suffering mother-in-law had been carefully informed about how "insulting" I had been. "But," I protested, "I didn't *mean* to be insulting. I did make a mistake—but I *don't* like sewing circles. When I sew, I like to tackle something huge, like a slip cover or draperies or a dress. I don't like to put a tea towel in a basket and sit and embroider all afternoon in somebody's living room!"

My defiance was short lived. At home I had always jokingly been called "the peacemaker" because I hated to quarrel on matters where principles weren't involved. I preferred peace, and if I had offended, however unintentionally, I was ready to make amends.

I called on the young woman I had offended, and by the time I got there was so nervous that I ended up in tears, promising to become a member of her club. For a whole year I did penance as I embroidered tea towels or some reasonable facsimile thereof one afternoon each week until a day came when I could graciously resign.

There were other episodes, equally silly and unimportant in retrospect, which somehow became major issues. I went through a good deal of grief before I realized why Jim was always so impervious to comment or criticism: it was really the only possible way to keep your own identity or peace of mind. But I still had that to learn.

Jim, when I fretted, answered equably, "Jane, is it really important? Don't fuss so over what people think or say. Your life is your own business. What you do with it is something between you and your God, not between you and your neighbors."

A good many of my difficulties, I know, were self-imposed, but I did *so* want to be a good wife and homemaker to the man I loved, and so often I despaired of ever succeeding. One of my troubles was trying to keep up with Jim's seemingly endless energy and enthusiasm.

"Jane, can you be ready at nine?" he would say, bounding from bed at dawn. "I want to show you the mill." (Or it was take a flying lesson, or take a group of Junior Endeavorers on a picnic, or whatever.)

"But Jim," I'd say desperately, "I've hardly touched this apartment, and I'm way behind on my correspondence. And when am I to get at the laundry?"

"Doesn't matter. No one expects you to do everything perfectly."

But *I* expected myself to do everything perfectly, and, while I always went with him, it was with a nagging sense of failure, of inadequacy. In particular I sensed that the ladies who came to call wondered at the disarray they found in our home —that small apartment which any woman "worth her salt" should have been able to clean in no time at all.

In my resolve to be a good wife, I determined to look out for Jim's health—not that there really seemed anything serious to worry about in that robust frame. But I knew he was supposed to be careful about his diet, though he paid so little attention to it. I decided that at home, at least, he was going to eat properly.

During my first weeks in Rockwood I went to Jim's family doctor and uncle, Dr. George Ed Wilson, to learn just what Jim could and could not eat. It turned out that Jim's diet consisted mainly of lean meats, eggs, fish, green vegetables, no fats, nothing fried, and no starches, one serving of fresh fruit at each meal—always fresh fruit, because at that time no sugar-free canned fruits were available.

By the time he was through with the list of what Jim could and could not eat, I was thoroughly depressed. I had already realized it was going to be quite a job to cook for him—but until just now, I hadn't realized what it would mean in terms of my own eating. I was extremely thin, and while I could eat all that Cotton was allowed to eat, I also needed a great many of the starches, sugars, and fats which Cotton couldn't take. It looked like a real "Jack Spratt" marriage—except that I knew I wouldn't eat what he could not eat at the same table with him.

I learned, too, that although there is no cure for diabetes, it can be controlled by daily injections of insulin. There was little comfort for me in this information, for Jim refused to go to all the bother of using insulin. It would be hard to keep Jim on any diet, for the lack of insulin in his blood deprived him of the nourishment he should have gotten from his food, and he suffered an abnormal craving for rich foods.

By the time I left the doctor's office, I was thoroughly worried. That very day I got a sharp taste of the problems I faced with Jim and his diet. Since I had spent most of the morning at the doctor's office, Jim would not have me try to fix lunch but insisted that we eat out instead.

He ordered for us both: fried chicken, mashed potatoes with gravy, green beans (Southern style—cooked for many, many hours with a slab of salt pork), apple sauce, and a lettuce and tomato salad. With the exception of the lettuce and tomatoes, everything on that menu was forbidden fruit so far as Jim was concerned. And when the salad came it was covered with a great gob of rich mayonnaise, also taboo. With the salad the waitress brought a basket of buttery corn sticks and a pitcher of water for Jim's enormous thirst.

I was dismayed, but Jim was oblivious. I could see him eating his way into an early grave. How on earth could I get him to change eating habits like these? I didn't want to start out by criticizing—and I didn't know whether he would listen.

But Jim made it easy for me. "How was your visit with Uncle George?" he asked.

I was grateful for the opportunity and I told him I'd gotten a list of what he was supposed to eat. "Jim," I added hesitantly, "this is not the kind of food you've been eating since we've been married."

"No," he admitted sheepishly. "I guess I've gotten pretty careless. I've just been eating here, there, and everywhere, and it gets pretty hard to stick to any kind of diet." He reached across the table and took my hand. "But *you* can help me. I'll get back on it again. Eating at home will make a lot of difference."

"And here we are eating at a restaurant!"

Jim shrugged and laughed. "This is only once. And it will really be a help to me. We'll be through early, and I can use the rest of my lunch hour to do some work on this month's Christian Endeavor bulletin." His voice took on its irresistible tone of enthusiasm. "I thought we could get a crowd together tonight right after supper to staple the sheets together and mail them. I think we'll have thirty-two pages this month, so it will be a big job."

And he helped himself to another corn stick, spread a pat of butter over it, and washed it down with half a glass of water.

The pace at which Jim lived and moved left me breathless, and at times a little frantic. But, as I was beginning to realize, his intense activity helped to keep his diabetes under control and helped to still the internal restlessness that often seemed to possess him. When circumstances kept him from being active, he was likely to come home ill. He would come in early from work, his usual ruddy color gone, his skin white and clammy to the touch, and admit he felt nauseated and drowsy. He would then drop into bed in the middle of the afternoon, to sleep heavily in a way that frightened me.

When I protested that he should do something about it, he passed it off as part of his disease. "It isn't important, Jane," he said. "I'll be all right tomorrow, and it just isn't worth taking time out." I wasn't at all convinced, but I didn't know what to do so I kept silent, feeling nonetheless much troubled about it.

Why I didn't share my personal troubles with Jim, I cannot now understand. But I did not. Our weeks assumed much of a pattern, on the surface gay and full and pleasant—I suppose much too full, for I never seemed to get through. The things we did together—flying lessons, church work, parties, calls—all were satisfying, but seemed to leave so little time for the things that were my own particular job. I never seemed to keep up with the apartment, and it was months before I finished writing all the notes of thanks for our wedding presents. Underneath, no matter what we were doing, I had a persistent, nagging sense of failure, of not measuring up, of being unable to fulfill my responsibilities.

The war ended that summer, and in the fall my brother came home to be married. I went to Florida the week before the wedding. Jim and I had been married five months, and this was the first time I had left him. It seemed to be a time to take stock, and to think about *us*.

Away from Jim's buoyant personality, I was most unreasonably depressed. I tried to hide my feelings for I didn't want to put a damper on the festivities, but with sharp parental eyes Mother noticed and asked what was wrong.

I tried to pass it off lightly. "Oh, I don't know. I guess just being away from Cotton."

Mother fussed at me, as mothers will. As soon as I could, I borrowed her car and escaped. Suddenly, now that I had admitted feeling depressed, I knew I had to think it all out. I drove down to the river and parked. The St. Johns was broad here, silvered now by the moon. Its shimmering surface was deceptively calm. Beneath the calm there was a swift current, driving out to the sea.

It seemed to me that my life was like this river I loved— glittering and lovely and deceptively calm on the surface, but underneath, a strong, swift current, whose destination I was unsure of. Against the joys of my life, the little frustrations were now overbalanced: the things which I had said or done wrong, the everlasting problem of Jim's health, the feeling of being always watched—and found wanting.

Even as I mentally listed my grievances, I knew they were trifling. Yet, they assumed a grotesque importance as I recited them and I couldn't stop. There was a hypnotic quality to this recitation. As the thoughts went round and round and round in my head, I felt as though I were sinking slowly and softly into an abyss. Around and down, down and around. No one could be such a fool as I—who else could agonize so endlessly over such little mistakes?

The path of the moon on the water was an alluring one. Suddenly the river which all my life had given me peace now seemed to beckon me to its depths. It would be so easy to swim out and out, to where the current grew swift, then just drift out to the wide, deep sea. . . .

In an instant, I realized where my thoughts were leading and was deeply shocked and ashamed.

To my mind came a long-familiar Bible verse: "There hath no temptation taken you but such as is common to man: but God *is* faithful, who will not suffer you to be tempted above that ye are able; but will with the temptation also make a way to escape, that ye may be able to bear it."

I sat there and thanked God for not letting me be the victim of my own weakness and folly. I just sat still and let the love of God sweep over me, recalling all the admonitions, all the assurances of God in time past: "Be strong, and of good courage," "Be not afraid, for I am with thee," "O taste and see that the Lord is good: happy is the man who trusts in Him."

In the thirty minutes since I had left the house, I had come through one of the major crises of my life. It had been a good while in building up, and had most certainly been built on trifles, but it is on trifles that many fail in life. I was going to have to do some reorganizing to manage my life better, but I knew that with God's grace, it could be done. I started the car, and backed away from the moonlit water.

Of course, I thought, there was a way out. If I had arrived at such a point of despair, even though it was my own fault, surely I could learn from it. If I couldn't talk to Jim about the way I felt, then I wasn't close enough to him. I hadn't given him a chance.

In the solitude of my room I wrote a letter to Jim, pouring out on paper the things I had been thinking, the experiences of that night. Some of the urgency must have come through in that letter, for Jim telephoned as soon as he received it. The connection was impossible, and I could hear almost nothing but static. At last, in exasperation, Jim shouted, "JANE, COME HOME!" That much I understood.

"All right," I answered meekly. "The wedding is tomorrow afternoon. I'll take a night train."

Jim was waiting for me at the station. He picked me up to whirl me about. "Jane, Jane, Jane," he said, "why didn't you *tell* me how you were feeling? How could I know? You didn't have to go so far away from me to tell me what you wanted. I love you, and I want to make you happy. Tell me when things trouble you—we can talk about anything."

And talk we did. Oh, the power of words to release the heart, to reassure the timid spirit! Now, in order to set my mind at rest, Jim seemed to come closer to me. Having seen my need, he changed in order to meet it, and he became more sensitive to my problems, more honest about my limitations. In the past months, it had sometimes seemed he had only left home briefly when he married—he had come right back to his own familiar place, and I had been the outsider trying to fit in, to adapt myself to his ways, his family, his town. Because I felt so alone, I had been hypersensitive to any comment or criticism.

From then on I was able to talk with Jim in complete freedom. This freedom to talk over what lies deepest in the human heart is perhaps the greatest single factor in a completely happy marriage. When you can talk about everything, you can't harbor resentment.

I am sure Jim didn't feel any such need of talk—he was quite self-sufficient, like most men, and reluctant to discuss or even put into words his inmost thoughts. But, understanding my need, he made a real attempt to help me—and as he did, he became steadily more articulate, more able to express himself fully. By giving to me, I honestly believe, he also gained.

Jim made another startling—and welcome—announcement the night I came home. "I told Uncle George we'd be down to see him," he said. "I'm ready to start taking insulin. We'll start taking care of my diabetes and see if I don't feel better, and you, too."

Chapter 4

As was his habit, Uncle George was laconic when we saw him. "Well, Boy," he said, "it's about time you made up your mind to start taking insulin. You've been ducking it for years, and I think you'll be a lot better off when you begin. But *I'm* not going to start you. You're too used to ignoring your family. I think you'll listen better to a stranger, and you ought to have a really complete physical anyhow. Let's see if my old friend Dr. Joslin in Boston can take you. If you're willing to go, Jane can go with you. Maybe you can both learn more about diabetes while you're there."

The cold in Boston was bone chilling. Dr. Joslin was conveniently at hand when we arrived at the New England Deaconess Hospital. He greeted us warmly and asked after Uncle George. He then went over the hospital procedure with us: Jim was to have a broad range of physical examinations and laboratory tests of all kinds. Then recommendations for treatment would be made, and dietary and insulin needs measured. In addition, we were both to attend classes for ten days to receive information on the daily care of diabetes at home.

I was honestly glad to leave Jim in the hospital and take a cab to my hotel. Fatigue from the long trip, the penetrating cold, and an odd physical malaise which had haunted me for some weeks made me quite ready—and thankful—to crawl into bed. I had never babied myself so before! At least there was no one to know but me.

The next morning, I was car-sick going out to the hospital. I wondered what on earth was wrong with me, then began to laugh as I realized the only possible answer. I had been nauseated every morning for four or five weeks, and had found fourteen different excuses to account for it. But there could only be one logical reason for all the recent "upsets." I hoped I was right in my diagnosis. I paid the cab driver and went up to Jim's room, feeling better than I had in weeks, in fact, almost floating on air. I could scarcely wait to tell Jim. He would be so proud and pleased.

He *was* pleased, but he had other things on his mind. When I reached his room, I found he had created a minor sensation by having the highest concentration of sugar in his blood of any patient ever to *walk* into the hospital. Everyone was amazed that he had never gone into a diabetic coma for lack of sufficient insulin.

The physical examinations were pretty much what we expected; we found the classroom lectures vivid and dramatic. We all learned how to give insulin with a hypodermic syringe —using water instead of insulin and an orange instead of a patient for our ham-handed experiments.

I had known that once Jim began to take insulin, he would have to take it for the rest of his life, receiving injections daily. I knew he had always hated the thought of this, and because I felt I had pushed him into it, I so hoped it would really be good for him, that he wouldn't mind it too much.

One morning after he had been in the hospital a week, I arrived to find him writing a letter to his mother. Simply to make conversation, I asked, "What are you telling her?"

"You read it."

I did, and to my surprise, he told her how marvelous it was to be taking insulin. "I was dying before," he said, "and didn't even know it, but this is like coming to life again. I can't imagine why I thought taking insulin would be dreadful and put it off for so long."

How wonderfully changed everything was in a few short weeks! I had a new relationship with Jim, his diabetes was now under control, and to top it off, I was expecting a baby! I checked with the gynecologist on Dr. Joslin's staff to make my suspicions a surety, and she was delighted with me. "We so seldom get to check a normal pregnancy," she explained. "It's nice to have one for comparison." It did not even upset me that I was still so miserably nauseated each day. I could largely ignore that in my present happiness.

At the end of two weeks all Jim's tests had been completed, his diet set up, his insulin intake regulated, and we were ready to go home.

Of course, we had to stop in New York. The trip down from Boston made me quite sick, and it would have been wonderful just to be quiet for a while, but this was not for me. Christmas was close and I felt obliged to find gifts for Jim's great family and my own. I went out to shop. For two deadly days I battled the crowds, the slush, and the cold. When I trudged wearily into the hotel the second afternoon, I wondered if I could summon the strength to leave our room again.

When I picked up the key at the desk, there was a note for Jim to call Rockwood as soon as he came in. I went on up, threw all my burdens into a chair, and without even taking off my coat or galoshes dropped onto the bed. The blessed relief of being able to lie *flat!* Without sitting up, I took a newspaper off the night table, and threw it to the end of the bed so I could lift my muddy feet up on it. That, I was sure, was the last effort of which I would be capable that day, and I just let go, hoping I could sleep.

Within fifteen minutes Jim came breezing in, with more bounce than a rubber ball. He saw me still in galoshes. "Hey, what's wrong," he said, "are you sick?"

"I think I've just had one crowd too many," I answered. "I'm afraid I'm only a country girl at heart. I'll be all right as soon as I rest a little. Oh, there's a message about a phone call. It's over there with my purse."

He found the note and picked up the phone. It took some time to get the call through, and I had almost drifted off to sleep when I heard him speak: "Yes, Bet? How bad is it? Is Mother all right? I'll see if we can't make the late train out of Washington tonight. That will put us in Knoxville tomorrow. Unless I phone again, have someone meet us."

I was fully awake again. "What was it?" I asked as he hung up the phone.

"Dad's had a stroke. It looks fairly serious, although he is comfortable at the moment. How soon can you be ready to leave?"

"Ten minutes. Oh, Jim, I'm so sorry."

We were able to get an early evening train to Washington, and rode into the worst blizzard in fifteen years. The cold had been bitter in the afternoon—now it was worse. Snow plows went ahead of the engine all the way, while our windows showed nothing but swirling whiteness. Fifteen minutes after leaving the station something happened to the heating system, and the miserable cold crept in upon us. We just made our connection, and with his usual finesse in getting people to do what he wanted, Jim arranged to have my berth made up at once. I was in it in a matter of minutes, but it seemed a very long trip to Knoxville.

Once home, I felt very sick, but was ashamed even to mention the way I felt. No one else I knew went to bed because they were pregnant, and I couldn't bear to be different, especially when Jim was so concerned about his father.

For a week, I put off going to Uncle George. By then, it was all I could do to get to the doctor's office. Uncle George was properly disgusted with me, and telephoned Jim to come get me and put me to bed. He told me not to move out of it, not even to sit up.

Jim came and *carried* me out to the car, and when we got home he *carried* me into the house. I was mortified. "Jim, this seems so silly!" I protested. "I've been walking around for weeks feeling this way."

"This is what husbands are for. Seems to me I promised to love and cherish you, and this is one way to do it."

Poor Jim. He divided his time between his job, his father, and me. He managed the mills and his visits to his dad in the daytime, then spent the evenings with me. He set up a card table and wrapped Christmas presents; we talked or he read to me through the long evenings. He found time during the day to stop by the library to find things he thought I would enjoy, and his thoughtfulness and patience brought a wonderful sweetness to our time together. As he held my hand each night while he said our evening prayer, my heart overflowed with love for him. At the end of each prayer, he added a hope that I might successfully carry the child we both wanted so much—but always he ended, "But *Thy* will be done."

Either I was too poor a patient, or we just weren't destined to have that child. I had more and more trouble, until I miscarried at the end of the second week.

"Well," I said, "I guess I ought to be glad it happened this way instead of possibly giving birth to a malformed child."

I had spoken more out of convention than conviction—but Jim took me up quite sincerely. "Good for you, Jane," he said. "That's exactly the way I feel, and I hoped you would see it that way." It was clear this was what he really felt. I think he had really wanted a child more than I did—he had certainly been almost bursting with pride ever since I had told him—yet when he was disappointed, he could accept it quietly and with no bitterness.

Inside, though, I didn't really look at it that way. I knew I should, but instead I felt hurt.

There are times when I can open my heart in prayer, and

these times are associated with an almost instantaneous sense of God's love and power and understanding. But there are other times when I can really only say words—there is in my spirit sometimes an inner core of rebelliousness which seems to close the door on God. It was so now. I said the words, I prayed for patience and wisdom and understanding, but there was no response, no kindling of the heart.

On the surface I tried not to show anything. But inside was the ache, the wish that it might have been otherwise. It was selfish to want more than I had, for my heart was full to over-flowing with the joy of our closeness these past weeks. It made me feel guilty.

That was the key: I *was* guilty. That was why I had found it difficult to pray. Until I came to the point where I could admit it, I only went through the motions of prayer. I realized I didn't see losing my child as the will of God, but as the quite natural consequence of my own folly: in a silly, unnecessary, and self-imposed martyrdom I had pushed myself beyond my strength, both before I was pregnant, and after.

I admitted a part of this to Jim, and he was too wise to deny it. "That may be so, dear, but you'll never know whether or not that was the deciding factor. Now, you mustn't fret. There's plenty of time for us. Just turn the past over to God, and leave it behind you."

Then I could pray and find comfort in it, "For He will abundantly pardon." When I asked for forgiveness, it was mine.

Jim's father grew gradually worse while I was in bed. He died the following March. Soon afterward, Jim and I moved into his mother's big house so she would not be alone.

Jim was elected to succeed his father as president of the company and his younger brother Woods, just out of the army, became vice-president. The Rockwood Mills were at that time one of the largest independent manufacturers of children's and men's hosiery in the world, employing about seven hundred people. Jim knew most of them intimately. He was interested in them and their welfare, and also in the effect of mill employment on the town's economy, for the mills provided the town's largest regular payroll. In all his business, Jim tried to keep these factors in mind, as well as his responsibility to the stockholders.

His life was geared to the rhythm of the mill whistle. He liked to be there before the night shift went off, and the day shift came on.

"If there's ever going to be trouble," he once explained, "it will be most likely to come then, through carelessness, when men are relaxed, some leaving and others arriving, when neither shift feels quite responsible, and when more people are on hand to be hurt in the event of an accident." He wanted to be there; it was important to him to be on the spot if he were needed. Fortunately, there was never a serious accident.

It didn't matter how he felt, it didn't matter where he had been the night before, or what else was happening, he was usually in the mill between six-fifteen and six-thirty in the morning. He made many out-of-town trips, either on mill or church business or a combination of both, but they were always very brief, so he was quickly home and at work again.

Though he discharged his business responsibilities faithfully and well, and although they might have occupied the whole life of another man, these duties were not the main interest in his life. Jim's greatest love was the church, for to it he gave most generously of his energy and time and money and enthusiasm. He was an elder in the Rockwood church, clerk of the session of the church, and for a time, superintendent of the Sunday school. He had worked widely for Christian Endeavor, and for years published the *Tennessee Christian Endeavorer,* a thirty to forty-page mimeographed bulletin for leaders and young people working in Christian Endeavor in the state. This was mailed to several hundred people every month, and was a mammoth job. Any of Jim's friends or the young people of the town were likely to find themselves at the mill after hours, working at the conveyor belt to assemble the pages, stapling them together and applying address labels.

But of all the jobs he did for or about the church, the one which meant the most to him was work with individual boys and girls. It seemed that the happier he was in his own life, the more he wanted to share his happiness. His care for each child was intense and personal and generous.

His projects for them were endless. Only through a wide multitude of life's experiences could you teach young people how to live, and each bit of time we spent with them gave us just that much more insight into their needs and opportunity to help them. I became just as deeply involved with them as he was. Nothing gave me greater satisfaction, and our work seemed to bring me even closer to Jim.

We pooled our talents and ideas, working sometimes together, sometimes separately. We worked together on all kinds of parties, hikes, treasure hunts, and the like. Jim specialized in athletics and work projects. I usually supervised service projects such as painting the Endeavor meeting room (which led the men of the church to go on and paint the rest of the church), making Christmas gifts and visiting. I did most of the story telling, and plays, and Christmas pageants.

One pageant I especially remember because of the angel. One sweet child, whom I shall call Betty, had her heart set on the part. "Please, Miss Jane," she asked me, "couldn't I be the angel this year?"

I looked in dismay at the little urchin before me. This wasn't the child I'd mentally chosen. Betty's dress was far too short, revealing spindly little legs grimed with the dust continually rising from the unpaved streets of Old Town, knobby little knees and elbows, her face streaked with dirt. And her hair— Oh, her hair! I wondered when it had ever truly been combed.

She'd made a stab at it—it looked as though a comb had been dragged through the top layer, but it was matted underneath and ragged at the ends.

It was her eyes that held me, though, for in them was the vision of Betty transformed into an angel, light and clean and shining and untouched by dust and grime. Seeing her vision, I knew it *had* to come true.

"Yes, Betty, you can be the angel."

There was no help to be expected from home. Her mother was often ill, and it was all she could do to keep her family fed, and some semblance of covering over their bodies. Such a luxury as a bath, in a two-room shack inadequately heated by one small oil stove and with no running water, was beyond her reach—but not beyond mine. "Betty, ask your mother if you can come home with me after the rehearsal the day before the play. I'll wash and cut and curl your hair if it will be all right with her."

Sure enough, following the long rehearsal the day before the pageant, Betty came to me. "Mama says I can go, Miss Jane."

We walked together in the twilight to our house. Betty's eyes were shining with happiness—she was going home with me, we were going to do something special together. She made me feel humble and ashamed. The little I could do for her would do nothing to lighten her poverty, and it was so very little out of my bounty.

I took her upstairs to the big old bath between our sitting room and bedroom, then went back down to the kitchen to get a tall chair so she could sit while I cut and shampooed her hair.

It took two hours. Her hair hadn't been washed in so long that it had become infested with lice. I wondered if I would ever be able to get them out of her tangled hair. It was the kind of horrible mess which should have been shaved off, but that would have humiliated the child—besides, she was to be the angel the next night, I had said so. So I forced myself to work at it patiently, cleaning and untangling a tiny bit at a time.

Poor little Betty grew weary—I hope she never knew how weary I grew. Jim came home, and I sent him to the drugstore for something to use when I got to washing it—I knew ordinary shampoo wouldn't suffice. Somehow I finished untangling and cutting her hair, then washed it three times. I trimmed it and shaped it and pinned it up in soft curls. I took her home with her hair still rolled up and a bright clean kerchief tied around her head. "The kerchief is yours, Betty," I told her. "You wear it to bed, then comb your hair out in the morning."

Once I had gotten through with the scrubbing part of the job, she had begun to brighten up, and looked up at me with joyous expectancy of the morrow, when she was to be the angel of glad tidings, high above the rest for once in her life, with a spotlight and five lines all her own.

I was crying by the time I reached home again. I scrubbed every inch of the bathroom and took all the towels down to the basement where I ran them through the washing machine twice with disinfectant—hoping I'd rid the house of every last "varmint."

When I got upstairs, it was long past our suppertime. Jim could see I was upset. "What is it, Jane?" he asked gently. "Betty looked very happy when she left. Did you mind doing it?"

"No. It was awful, but I didn't mind doing it. But it'll be almost as bad again in three days. Isn't there *something* we can do about them?"

"Not really much more than you're doing. You can teach her to want cleanliness, and you can teach her how to do for herself—but you can't do much more. If you take her good clothes, her father will take them away and sell them for drink. He had a really bad time during the depression, and though he's really making a fair enough salary just now it all goes to the bottle. The mother could put the children in the parental home near Knoxville. But she has her pride, and she'd never see them so far away—and who are you or I to interfere?"

He was right, but it seemed so unfair, so dreadful that in this land of abundance and plenty any child should have such lack. Yet all we could really do was win their hearts, teach them the best we knew, and love them through the years of their lives.

There were so many and their needs were so great. In the Junior group, the children were just emerging from the family circle into the larger world beyond school and home, and needed especially to feel there were adults beyond their parents and teachers who had a real interest in them and in their progress.

In the Junior High group, there were all the problems of adolescence—and for the boys more than for the girls, the problem of decision. Our children came to Christian Endeavor for many reasons. A few came because their parents told them to come. Some came for the fellowship of the group, some for the parties, some for the swimming season because they knew we would take them regularly and teach them how to swim. Some came because we picked them up in our car, and it was the only time in the week they had a chance to ride in an automobile. But whatever their reasons, they soon learned that none of these things was the most important thing about Christian Endeavor.

Bit by bit, week after week, line upon line, verse upon verse, precept upon precept, they became acquainted with their Bibles, with Christ, with the Christian way of life. Inevitably, they were forced to a decision, because these glimpses of Christ and His Way made them question other ways— and since some ways were irreconcilable, there had to be a choice made.

For the Juniors, it was easy. They were at the age of hero

worship, and Jim was a convenient hero. What he believed they accepted as truth without question. With the Junior Highs it was different. At their age, to stand alone is the most difficult thing in the world. Yet the patterns to which they were expected to conform in their school and social life didn't always jibe with what they had learned at Christian Endeavor. This raised questions. *Was* the Christian way of life the best? If it was, why didn't more people live it? There were a few, like Jim and Dr. Orr—but if you weren't rich like Cotton, or a minister like Dr. Orr, what then? What did it get you? Was it worth it?

We never wanted these decisions to be hurried or forced. Yet it was usually easy to see when they were coming— though not always possible to know which way they would decide. There was always a restlessness, usually many leading questions. Sometimes it was just a look of longing, almost indefinable, which bespoke the hunger of the heart. We prayed for all of them frequently, but when we sensed that this urgency of deciding was upon them, then we simply "lifted them up in prayer" whenever we thought of them.

For some time a boy whom I'll call Ben lay upon my heart in this way. He was just fourteen, a slender boy with a dark sensitive face. His mother was a great phlegmatic woman who always seemed to have a new baby at her ample breast, and his father an inoffensive little man whose only achievement had been to sire this great brood. Ben was the oldest child in a stair-step family. He was intelligent and thoughtful, and his decision mattered a great deal to me. There was something about him that drew me, and kept him in my consciousness so that I prayed for him a great deal.

He hesitated for some time. He would come to meetings because they satisfied some hunger in him, then he would stay away to show he had no need of the meetings or of us. We made no effort to push or pull in either direction, until the time came for the annual youth meeting.

This had been started some years before when our friend Tom Scott was head of the Youth Council of Rockwood's Council of Churches, and had been continued each year. It was really a series of five or six meetings during Christian Endeavor–Youth Week at the end of January, when all the young people of all the churches met to hear some particularly inspiring or outstanding speaker and song leader. At the end of the meetings, there was traditionally a time for those who wished to rededicate their lives to Christ to come forward and do so at the altar, and for those who had never made a public confession of faith to come forward and do so. Some objected to this public confession of belief in Christ, but we felt it was part of Christ's plan, for He said, "Whoso will confess me before men, him will I confess before my father which is in heaven."

"Do you think Ben will come to the meetings?" Jim asked.

"I don't know. He's troubled, and I think it will help him—but I also think it would be the wrong time for you or me to speak to him. There is no age so independent as fourteen."

"I know. We'll just hope."

It was rare for Jim and me to sit together in church. He was usually singing in the choir, assisting at a baptism, or helping to serve the Communion. He had no such special duties at these meetings, and it was pleasant to sit by him and share his hymnbook. I looked up when he squeezed my hand, and followed his gaze. Ben had come in and seated himself at the side of the church. He came each night, just a little late, as if he didn't want to speak to anyone, and slipped away quickly afterward, as if he really didn't want anyone to know he had been there.

On the fourth night, however, he didn't slip away. When the invitation was given, Ben stepped out of his pew and walked confidently down the aisle to kneel before the altar. Once more, Jim's hand sought mine and held it tightly. We needed no words to convey our feelings to each other.

We had no illusion that Ben was now set in his Christian faith. He was just a boy, bound and limited in many ways. But he had, in that moment toward which he had been building for some time, been willing to stand forth in his declaration of faith in Christ as the Son of God, and to pledge allegiance to Him.

Jim and I talked of this afterward. "Whatever happens to Ben," Jim said, "this will forever serve him as a point of identity. If only we had more time to give him, time to be with him, and help him become stronger in his faith, he might have less chance of losing this little insight. Jane, sometimes it seems we fritter our lives away, spreading ourselves so thin there isn't a quarter of the time we ought to be spending on the really important things!"

Chapter 5

I WENT TO FLORIDA to visit my mother the second summer we were married. It was quite different from my previous troubled trip. This time we missed each other dreadfully, and I was never able to leave Jim again for more than a few days. He stood his loneliness for three weeks, then came after me.

Our marriage had become richer and deeper. Never had I been more happy. Jim was in all things the head of his household—yet he managed to impart the feeling that my being close to him was absolutely essential to his well-being and happiness.

I believe that "confirmed" bachelors make the best husbands. After years of thinking single bliss is the only kind, the revelation of a happy marriage gives them a feeling that *their* marriage, *their* love is a thing to be especially treasured.

I loved to see Jim look up and smile because I had come into the room where he was. He was an ardent and affectionate husband, and liked to be aware of my nearness. If I were close by, he liked to know it, and if I were close enough, he would always reach out to touch me in some way. I made a point of being where he could reach me if he wanted to.

There were just two things lacking in our life. The first was children of our own. In one sense, we had many children, but the depths of human love are never really plumbed—I wanted at least one or two of our own.

47

The other thing I wanted was a home of our own. In a way, it seemed a silly wish, for it was comfortable and convenient to live with Jim's mother, and it gave me a good deal of freedom. Yet in the secret places of my heart the wish grew into a longing, so passionate it was almost irrational, for a home I could call mine.

Jim wanted a home, too, though not, perhaps, with the same deep yearning as mine. We had decided that when we built our own home, we wanted it to be on the lake created by the TVA dam near Rockwood. Canoeing one day, we were delighted with one particular hill we found on its shores. We beached our canoe in the sandy-bottomed cove at its base and climbed the well-worn meandering cow path up the hill to see what was on top.

When we reached the top, we were breathless, both from the effort of the climb, and from the magnificent view. The woods ended abruptly at an abandoned peach orchard high up, and at the summit was a clearing which gave an unimpeded view in every direction.

When he had caught his breath Jim said softly, "The heavens declare the glory of God; and the firmament sheweth His handiwork."

Below us spread a panorama of the Tennessee River, twisting down from Kingston in the north and broadening out into Watts Bar Lake in the south. Far to the northeast, the foothills of the Smokies rose dimly on the horizon. To the west beyond Rockwood, which lay hidden from our sight by a hill, Waldens Ridge cut off the late-afternoon sun. In between, smaller hills separated the valleys and held back the river.

We wanted it. We found the owner, a farmer named Jim Pierce, and over a period of months dickered over it. At last we bought a hundred and ten acres of land, including the coveted hilltop. Then we went ahead, and drew up a simple plan to which we could add later.

First we had to have a road. From the county road to the

top of our hill, we found a mile-long dirt track, which had been used by trucks when the orchard was producing. We had the full mile graded and gravel poured on, truckload after truckload.

Materials were hard to find, and the building went slowly. But when at last it was ready, it was beautiful: very simple and unpretentious—just one huge room paneled in knotty pine, with a high, arched ceiling, a handsome fireplace flanked by bookcases, and wide expanses of glass so we could enjoy the view. There was a bath and a tiny kitchen which would later be a closet.

When we built, no one lived on the lake except a few farmers. As soon as we began our house, everyone asked, "Why are you going to live 'way out there?" "What are you going to *do* all day?" "Won't you be lonely?"

The questions seemed absurd to me. My problem all my life had been to find time enough to do the things I wanted to do. Like Jim, I was a bit of an enthusiast. My enthusiasm ran to feminine things: I sewed a great deal, hooked rugs, painted, knitted and crocheted. I loved to read, wrote letters to my many friends and my family. And how I enjoyed the blessed solitude!

I had learned to love Rockwood, but there were times when I just wanted to be alone. Here, we always had people in, but it was a rare day when I wasn't entirely alone for a few hours. Then I could work on whatever foolish or worthwhile project I chose, without explaining it to everyone. There wasn't even a telephone.

Jim's part in acquiring our home had been more acquiescent than enthusiastic. Knowing my eagerness to have a house, he had been willing from the start to create one for me, and had helped through the long months of collecting materials and poring over plans. But I had been afraid that he might be irked by the responsibilities of the house, rather than pleased. I needn't have worried. From the time we moved in, he assumed the role of "country gentleman" with that complete and boundless enthusiasm which he gave to every new project which caught his fancy.

In honesty, I must admit that he applied to it all more mind than muscle. Meanwhile our vast acreage remained covered with dying peach trees, sagebrush, persimmon and sassafrass "volunteers," black walnuts, and wild blackberries. One little boy commented with mock innocence, "Mr. Huff can grow the best blackberries of anybody." Nobody enjoyed the joke more than Mr. Huff, since they just grew.

For a while, I thought Jim might become really interested in farming. One fine spring morning, he rode into town and saw that the farmers on every hand were plowing their fields and planting crops. He had by now done about all the reading he could, and decided the day had come to till the soil. He hired a man to cut brush and plow some fields, and he came home with a bushel of seed potatoes.

Painstakingly, he cut the potatoes into sections, and walked down the plowed rows dropping in the pieces and covering each one with soil. Never had I thought I would see the day!

He brought home seed corn and between the rows of corn, he planted pumpkins. The potato vines came up rich and thick, the corn flourished. The pumpkin vines traveled along between the rows of corn, produced a number of yellow blossoms which scarcely shriveled before they were followed by tiny green balls.

Jim was enraptured. He had always been reluctant to do so much as dig a hole in the ground to plant a rose bush. But now he had seen green vines and cornstalks from seed he had planted, he hung over them as a new father haunts the nursery. He went down to look at his fine fields at dawn each morning and could scarcely wait to get home in the evening to see how much they had grown during the day.

As the season advanced, though, he had to sacrifice his enjoyment of the growing potatoes to organize and outfit a troop of Boy Scouts for a trip to the Jamboree at Valley Forge. Raising boys, after all, was more important than raising potatoes, and I was all in favor of his decision. He was busy every minute, though, with plans and work for the trip, and his beloved fields had to be neglected.

I was willing to take over many of the land duties, but some jobs were just too much for me!

"Jane," Jim threatened, "if I don't get time to do it, you're going to have to spray my potatoes."

"Jim," I replied, "I don't *want* to spray any potatoes!"

I did wonder if I should, though. Certainly Jim had no time for it. Well, if he didn't have time, I rationalized, let him arrange for someone else to do it!

He saw to every detail but the spraying before he left. Ten days later my sister Martha came up for the weekend and asked if it wasn't time for us to have some nice new potatoes.

"I don't know," I replied. "I haven't been down there since Jim left."

Martha volunteered to walk down the hill and look.

A few minutes later she was back, her face downcast. "Jane," she said, "you really should have sprayed those vines. There isn't a single one left on the whole hillside."

"Oh, dear," I said, "they were so pretty when Jim went away." I was truly chagrined. I knew Jim would come home bursting with pleasure over his trip, anxious to know how his garden had done in his absence. I hated to tell him all his potatoes had died while he was out tending to other people's children. I could at least have done my share at home. But then I thought how much work it was to spray potatoes by hand and realized that even if I'd known what would happen, I still wouldn't have done differently. Vain regrets couldn't bring back his beloved vines, so there was nothing to do but tell him when he came.

Jim was a good loser, and when he heard the news, he only shrugged his shoulders. At least there was still the corn, and the pumpkins, and the potatoes had been sacrificed to a good cause.

A couple of weeks later one of our friends had a birthday, and we went to help celebrate the occasion. There were half a dozen other couples, all good farmers, and somehow Jim had occasion to tell about the potatoes I hadn't sprayed. They all began to roar with laughter. One man finally wiped the tears from his eyes and asked, "Did you dig under them dead vines?"

No, we hadn't. They were dead, why dig?

This got another round of laughter. "You go home and dig," we were told.

By now we suspected why they were laughing, but we could scarcely wait to get home and *see*. Jim was so curious he couldn't wait for daylight. He got a spading fork, handed me a flashlight, and we went down to the field. I held the light while he turned the earth. In the dim light, we couldn't be sure whether he was turning over rocks or potatoes, but picking one up, shaking off the dirt, we were convinced.

Those vines had done their work, and in the fullness of time had withered and died. The bugs hadn't harmed Jim's crop at all—hidden in the earth was a bountiful harvest, waiting to be reaped. Jim dug potatoes every spare minute until frost. We lugged heavy sacks of them to all our relatives and friends and still had enough left to last us all winter.

No farm would be complete without animals, and Jim soon bought some for us. He gave me three hundred chickens and a hideous chicken house. He found some suckling pigs at a price too low to resist and nursed them along. It seemed to me we spent everything we had in buying food for those pigs. They grew and ate, ate and grew, grew and ate, but mostly ate!

Jim wanted to breed his own pigs, but his farmer friends persuaded him it wasn't worth the trouble. From one of them he purchased a purebred Poland China sow, almost ready to farrow. The thought of buying one pig and having it produce ten more so fascinated Jim that one sow led to another, also ready to farrow.

However, while he wasn't particularly squeamish, it somehow always worked out that just about the time those sows were due, Jim had a most important trip to New York or Chicago. A mere litter of pigs could hardly compete with a large order or work for the church or Christian Endeavor: off he would go, leaving me to play midwife to the sow.

I can't recall a single litter that arrived in broad daylight. I would never have minded, except that they always came after dark, preferably in the midst of torrential rain. Nor was the sow ever in the farrowing pen when her time came. Always, she found a way out and off down the hillside. Like a wild creature she would make a nest of sorts, rolling in the underbrush until it was crushed beneath her weight. She would continue rolling as she gave birth to her litter, then as she made herself comfortable afterwards. Most of the newborn piglets were crushed if someone wasn't on hand to rescue them as they arrived.

This was one of the times in life when I most vehemently detested my Scotch and New England ancestry. Surely any sane person could crawl comfortably into bed, forget the pigs, and sleep the night through in peace. Not I. In the night and the wind and the rain and the darkness, I was out tramping the woods with only a lantern for company.

Once Jim managed to be on hand for the great event. On a late November afternoon when Dilly (I couldn't resist giving the foolish creatures names) was due, we went down together in the gray twilight to check on her. We had coaxed her up into the farrowing pen the day before, and she was getting restless in the confined space.

"I think we've got it fixed so she can't get out this time," Jim said after checking the pen.

"I hope so," I said dubiously, "but she's really thrashing

about, and I don't think the pen will last another twenty-four hours under that punishment."

"Why twenty-four hours?" Jim asked.

"I'm sure it'll be late tomorrow before that litter arrives," I replied drily. "You're always safely away from here when they come, and your train doesn't leave until noon tomorrow. Therefore. . . ."

Jim laughed. "Jane, don't be so hard on me. I don't plan it that way."

"I think your subconscious has something to do with it. Someday, though, you're going to have to help deliver those pigs."

The wind seemed to be rising, and the cold had a raw, damp bite to it. Inside, we shed our coats and galoshes. It was the kind of night when the house seemed especially secure. I had lighted a fire, and the coals were glowing. The table was set before the fire, and Jim put a stack of records on the phonograph. We lingered over supper. There was a seductive charm in the firelight seclusion, so far from the cares and bustle of town. I knew it must be growing colder outside, and suddenly realized it was also raining.

"Mercy, how long has it been raining?" I asked Jim. "I didn't hear it begin."

"Quite a while. I'm thinking I'd better go down and see if Dilly is all right. She seemed so restless."

The wind seemed to suck at the door when he opened it, and I was glad *he* was home to do the checking.

He was back in a couple of minutes, and stood with his back against the door, dripping. His face was rueful. "Looks like I'm caught this time. Dilly's broken out. What do I do now? I'll never be able to get her back up the hill in this storm."

I made a face at him. "And I was just rejoicing because my hero was here, and I wouldn't have to go out in the storm!"

I put on a sheepskin-lined jacket, a woolen hood, and my

galoshes, then picked up the other flashlight. "This is just the kind of night for it. I think I'll take a basket, too. We might be able to herd Dilly up after the blessed event, but we'll have to tote the litter."

With the wind at our backs, we walked to the pen. One wall of the pen yawned outward, where mere lumber and nails had proved no match for six hundred and fifty pounds of thrashing pig. Her path through the brush was plain enough, each hoof print filled with water—but it was soon apparent we couldn't follow. Every branch was laden with water, waiting only a touch to loosen its load upon us.

"We'll never make it this way, Jim," I cried. "Let's go round to the path, I think I know where she'll be holed up."

Once we stepped down the path, the friendly lights of the house were swallowed by darkness. The hillside gave partial shelter from the wild wind, but above us the trees were shaken back and forth, loosing sudden showers and creating a strange and primitive world. The wind has always seemed to me a special sign of God's presence and power, and I have always faced it with a quickening of the senses and spirit.

We had gone some distance down the hill when Jim cautioned me. "Stop," he said. He listened a moment, "She's over this way. We'll have to go through the brush."

We beat our way off the path, until we found her.

"Foolish Dilly," I reproached her. "Why couldn't you stay where it was sheltered?"

"Just like a woman," muttered Jim in a tone I was intended to hear.

"If it weren't dark, I'd stick my tongue out at you."

Dilly had just delivered herself of a small, squirming, pink baby pig, which Jim snatched up, carefully keeping clear of the snorting wild-eyed sow. He held it in the light a moment. Weighing perhaps two pounds, hairless, it looked quite raw and blind. It was already beginning to wiggle and twist its tiny snout in an instinctive search for food. It fit quite comfortably in Jim's big hand. He laid the little pig tenderly in the basket, and I covered it with a tarpaulin.

By the time we had Dilly and her offspring safely bedded down for the night, the storm was over. A waning moon shone down on us through sky frothed with small puffy clouds scudding swiftly northward. We pocketed our lights and walked up to the house hand in hand, satisfied and content. We had won the battle: we had outwitted the foolish sow, and had saved every one of her soft little pigs from her clumsiness. In our hearts was that lift which comes with the miracle of birth, and a little of the sentimentality and yearning which dwells in those of us who have never given birth to young of our own.

Jim's success at farming was gratifying for us both. We could afford the lime and fertilizer which made our land productive. But to our sorrow, this was not the case with many of our neighbors. There was a meagerness and poverty throughout the area which pulled at the heart, both on the farms and among the town workers.

Jim drove up to the house one Saturday afternoon, about three.

"What happened?" I called from the door. "Couldn't you find a soul who would tolerate you for an afternoon of golf?"

He kissed me as he came in and told me quietly that a child, whom I shall call Willy Jones, had died at noon over in Clymerville. "They just thought he had a cold, but it must have been pneumonia. Poor little tyke, by the time they decided someone had better go for the doctor, it was too late. Can you get some chickens out of the freezer and fry them? We ought to take something out to the house."

I thawed the chickens in hot water, dipped them in a mixture of salt, pepper, and flour, and fried them a crisp brown. I lined a cardboard carton with foil and packed the chicken in it so there would be no plate to be returned.

Jim briefed me as we drove into town. "You've only met

part of his family, Jane. His daddy came to church once or twice, and his grandmother was always there. His mother died when Will was two." Jim could outline the least branches on the family tree of any person in the area.

We drove through Rockwood, then out the dirt road past the slag dump to the poor little cluster of houses which made up Clymerville. Most of the houses in Clymerville backed on the mountain, and they were perched on high stilt-like foundations which looked all the more fragile and pitiful against the solidity of the hillside.

The house before which we stopped sat alone, but was identical to the others farther down the road. There was a steep flight of wooden steps, a porch with a single rail, and an unscreened door leading into the main room. Jim took the carton of fried chicken, and we walked up the steps.

On the porch were all the men of the neighborhood, chatting softly. Jim opened the door for me and gave the chicken to a woman who came forward to greet us. I had been in the house before, when this room had contained two iron bedsteads, several chairs, and a high table on which were grouped the family photographs. Now, the beds had been taken away and the chairs lined the wall, augmented by twelve or fifteen folding chairs from the funeral parlor. In these sat the ladies from the neighborhood and from the church, whispering quietly.

The windows had been darkened, and it took a few moments to take in the details of the room. The thin single floor with its worn oilcloth rug in the center was shining—evidence of a pride that fights to overcome poverty. At one end of the room was the coffin.

One look at it made me ill. My first thought was, "The boys really sold them the works!" There lay Willy, who probably never had a new pair of shoes in all his life, but had worn the castoff shoes and neatly mended clothing his brother had outgrown.

What his family hadn't been able to give Willy in this life, though, had been rashly spent on him now, when Willy had no use for it. I supposed they would be in debt for years to pay for the fine casket in which Willy was "laid out." It was burnished metal with elaborate handles. The inside was lined in white velvet, yards and yards of it, and there was a velvet cushion for poor Willy's head.

On either end of the casket were grotesque electric torch lights supplied by the funeral home, and above all, a deep-toned, fringed, velvet canopy—strangely incongruous beneath the raw beams of the unceiled roof.

An unctuous little funeral attendant took hold of my arm in a way that was far more personal than helpful. I shook him off, and stood with Jim while he signed the visitors' register. Jim was the only one in the room to use a natural tone of voice. He spoke to the women who were there—who answered in funereal whispers. He then asked for Willy's grandmother, and went back to the bedroom to see her.

"Jane," he said, "you sit here and wait for me."

Dr. Orr had died in the spring of 1947, and we were temporarily without a minister. Jim probably knew the family better than anyone else in the church did, and as an elder was the natural one to go to comfort them. I knew he would be gone for a while.

I did not know the woman next to whom I sat, but I shall never forget her. She had a harsh, sharp whisper—and she felt she had to whisper in that room, so I heard only snatches. It was one of the few times in my life when I wished I were stone deaf instead of just slightly incapacitated.

There was no way to escape. I was compelled to wait there for Jim, as I could hardly go out on the porch with the men. So I sat, trying to maintain a courteous expression. The woman spoke with obvious relish.

"I thought that child was right sick . . . told them he'd need doctorin' . . . his ma looked like that when she was took . . .

that kind of constitution runs in families . . . I told her I'd go down to the Hayes . . . only phone out here . . . funeral parlor . . . I went right back with them, I wasn't going to have them men wash that little boy, I did it myself . . . you never know what they'll do if you ain't watchin' . . . I stood right there while they . . . then I dressed him myself just the way you see him now. . . ."

It was a tremendous relief when Jim came out of the bedroom, nodded to the ladies, and took my hand to lead me out. I was terribly depressed. "Jim, it was so awful," I protested.

"Yes, baby," he agreed. "It was."

It had grown much colder by the time we reached home. We rode up the hill in the last of twilight, and walked into the house together in a thoughtful silence as full darkness enveloped us. Jim patted my shoulder lightly, and walked on to light the lamps in the living room.

At the click of the switch, the room was bathed in radiance. The softly rubbed paneled walls, the polished oak flooring, the gentle heat that enveloped us—all this was so shockingly different from the house we had just left that I shivered involuntarily.

It was true, I had finished the floors myself and carefully waxed the walls to their present sheen—but I hadn't really had to. It just made the contrast all the more terrible.

"Jim, oh, Jim," I cried. "Why is life so hard for some people? That farce we just went through was the final indignity! There wasn't money enough to call the doctor—yet they were talked into a casket which must have cost enough to have fed and clothed the whole family for a year. Then that morbid witch was gloating over all the details of preparing the body so people could come and gawk at it and say how 'natural' he looked. As if there were anything natural about a body from which the life and spirit were gone. When I die, you get the cheapest box you can buy to put my body in, and nail the lid on. I don't want anyone combing the hair and painting the face I've left behind so a lot of morbid souls can peer at it and say I look 'natural!' "

Jim had put his arms around me during my outburst. "I know, Jane, I know," he said soothingly. "I feel the same way. But you're not going to change customs by getting all wrought up over them. Most people, even Christians, are frightened and insecure when they face death. They simply don't understand that death merely frees the soul from the body, so it may be with Christ. That's why they grasp so pitifully at any gesture when someone they love dies."

"It seems such a tragic waste," I said, "To make such a burden of burial."

"True," Jim said, then went on partly in jest, but more than half in earnest, "by the time of my funeral, I hope I'll have been in Heaven for three days. In fact, instead of a funeral, I'd like to have a party given for me. I've lived all my life in the expectation of being received into Heaven as soon as I draw my last earthly breath—and I don't want anyone crying for me. It should be a time of great rejoicing—*unless*," he added mischievously, "my course has so changed that it seems evident I couldn't have gotten into Heaven at all. If you think I've gone to the other place, why then you *should* mourn!"

I laughed, but knew he meant what he said.

"If you die before I do," he went on, "I'm going to have you buried up on the hill. But I'll never go up there again, because you won't be there." Then he went on earnestly, "But if I go first, don't grieve. Learn to use God's strength and love to carry you through your loneliness, then build a whole new life for yourself. Stay active and busy, and marry again if you can. If God takes me first, then I'm sure He means for you to do just that."

"It's hard to imagine, Jim," I said, deeply moved. "At least I'll remember what you've said, and I'll try."

"Good," he said, smiling. "We're a long way short of the twenty-five years I promised you. You know I love you too much to leave you if I can help it, or to let you leave me either.

"I sometimes wish, though," he said, "that I could spend my life assuring people that in the love of God, they need have no fear of death."

Chapter 6

SEVERAL DAYS after this, Jim came home with the news that they had had an offer from a large corporation to buy the hosiery mills.

At first I was shocked. "Surely you'd never give it up!" I said. "It's your life!"

"It's not all my life," he said quietly. "And it would probably be a mighty good thing for the stockholders. They would get three to one on their original investment, while we'd have to do a lot of scratching in order to continue declaring regular dividends. We need new machines and renovation, and with taxes the way they are, we can't get up enough capital to do the job properly. But these folks have plenty of capital for new machinery, and they ought to be able to keep the mills running even through a depression. I'm afraid that's more than we could count on doing." He went on enthusiastically, describing the benefits to the stockholders and the workers if the business were sold. It sounded as if he really wanted to get out. I was flabbergasted.

"But Jim, what would *you* do?" I asked. "Would that mean the end of your job?"

"I don't know just what I'd do," he replied. "It seems to me we ought to look at it just from the point of view of the stockholders and the mill workers. There'll always be something for me."

"But Jim," I persisted, "if the sale does go through, what will really happen to you?" And, womanlike, I might have added, *"How will it affect me?"*

"Oh, baby, there are lots of possibilities. I might stay on and work for the new company if they wanted me, or I might organize a small mill of my own. There's plenty of time to think about it."

He didn't sound so enthusiastic about this. Obviously something else was on his mind. I had often wondered what he would have chosen to do if he hadn't inherited the family business. "But, Jim, what would you most like to do? What would you do if you were starting life all over?"

"Oh, that's easy, honey. I'd go into the ministry. That's what I should have done twenty years ago."

There it was. Suddenly I realized the secret yearning in his heart. I knew what he wanted.

"Why don't you go ahead and do it now?" I asked.

He dismissed the idea at first. "Jane, that's silly. I'm almost forty, and it's too late to go back to school. I still lack two years of college, and that would mean five years of school before I could even begin to serve. No, honey," and he seemed to hesitate before the painful words. "I'm too old."

But the idea persisted. He returned to it several times in the days that followed. "It really seems absurd," he said, "but I keep thinking about it. Lately, I've had the feeling I haven't done as much with my life as I could have, and I think this would be the most satisfying way to spend the rest of it. I feel I've been so blessed myself that I'd like a way to share my blessings with others."

We even began to talk practically about it. We discussed the sum his own shares of mill stock would bring. We could probably get something for the farm where we were living. We had no savings, for we had always lived up to our income, but we began to plan, to make budgets to see if we could possibly swing the long session of schooling.

The more we planned, the more enthusiastic we grew. I knew I could stay within any reasonable budget. With care, we could make it through the school years and still have a small backlog for emergencies when we had to live on a minister's salary. Our plans gave us an exhilarating sense of adventure.

Negotiations for the mill continued, my hopes soared, and Jim began to grow impatient. Then, just when we felt everything was ready, the negotiations bogged down. In a few days, Jim came home with a long face.

"Honey," he said ruefully, "I guess God didn't think much of the idea of me as a minister. The sale is definitely off. That seems to be a clear indication that He did not mean for me to go. I guess it was just an idealistic dream."

Meanwhile our life went on in its accustomed round, and other concerns took up our attention.

We had been married four and a half years, but I still kept hoping we would have a child. I was elated when I began suffering morning nausea. When I went into Rockwood to see Uncle George, he confirmed my hope. He gave me a special diet to follow, and a prescription for my nausea. Uncle George was cheerful about my condition, and Jim and I were overjoyed. *This* time, I thought, I could make it through the full nine months.

But within weeks, despite all our precautions, complications arose. The worst of it was that the day I was taken ill, Jim was to leave on a business trip to Chicago. I was so worried and ashamed that I couldn't bear, I thought, to call attention to my illness, so I urged Jim to go ahead with his trip and tell no one. Of course, it meant that I would be stranded in the country with no car or phone, but I didn't care.

Jim was most reluctant to leave me, but there was nothing he could do, for I wouldn't have him stay. However, before he left he told his brother Woods that I was having trouble.

Woods told his mother, and she sent him out forthwith to check on me.

I had gone to sleep as soon as Jim left, and wakened to Woods' knock. The sleep had restored my sense of well-being, and there was no further sign of trouble.

Woods wanted me to stay in town while Jim was gone, but the little respite had sent my hopes soaring. I told him I didn't want to ride over the country roads. I just might make it if I stayed quietly in one place.

Woods shook his head over me. He had lived all of his life completely surrounded by his kin, and could in no way understand my need for solitude. That I should wish to be alone "at a time like this" was completely beyond his comprehension. He decided to go back and see what his mother and Uncle George thought should be done.

I knew a family conference would be held—I fear my whims and vagaries were a trial to them all. More than an hour passed. Relieved, I decided they were going to let me be. I was propped up in my chaise longue, watching the sun set over the distant mountains when I saw what looked like a hearse coming slowly out the "Jiney Holler" road. The thing disappeared from view, moving down the country road. I thought no more of it—until it reappeared again, toiling up the last of our road. It *was* a hearse!

"My, my," I thought. "What is this for?" Woods got out, accompanied by two long-faced men bearing a stretcher. As they made for my front door, there was absolutely no doubt that they had come for me.

I didn't dare giggle. I knew if I gave way to my impulse to laugh, they would be sure I was insane. Woods said gravely that I was to be taken to the hospital at once and was not to walk another step. The stretcher bearers advanced into my living room and stared at me speculatively. I knew any protest would be futile. These two stalwart fellows had been hired to lug bodies, and I could tell that was what they were going to do. I awkwardly laid myself down on the stretcher and was borne out to the waiting hearse.

The driver did his best to make an easy ride over our miserable excuse for a road, but he might as well have taken his foot off the brake and let us go lickety-split down the hill. Stretched out full length, I felt every bump, stone, and rut we rolled over.

At the foot of the hill, the usually deserted road was lined with people on either side. As the hearse had rolled toward our house, the word spread like ripples on a quiet pond. People laid aside whatever they were doing and came to our road in sympathy or curiosity, to wait for the hearse and see whether its burden was living or dead. To make the point clear, I waved gaily at them all, feeling like a ham actor in a badly written melodrama. (Jim explained later that the ride was *gratis*. "They charge it up to advertising," he explained, "and figure they're going to get you in the end.")

At the hospital, I still felt foolish as they moved me from the hearse to my hospital room—but I knew sadly that I *was* ill, and would *not* have this child either.

Jim's mother was seething with indignation because he had left me, and furthermore, had left me in the country with neither car nor telephone.

"But I *told* him to go," I insisted. "He is very considerate when I'm ill and worries much more than I do."

"That's no excuse at all," she snapped. "A husband is supposed to be with his wife at a time like this!"

There was really no way to explain to her how I felt, especially since I knew her anger stemmed from her sincere concern over me. But my heart bled for Jim, since I knew he would suffer even more when he heard.

Of course, they called him, but I didn't expect him so soon. Suddenly there he was in the doorway of my hospital room, and then he was kneeling beside the bed, his arms around me.

"Jane, Jane, Jane," he whispered, "I shouldn't have gone. You know how much I love you—and you made it so easy for me to believe you'd be all right. I shouldn't have left you alone."

How could I say what was in my heart? *"Oh, Jim, you shouldn't be apologizing to me. How can I tell you how it breaks my heart not to give you children, the children you would love so much? And now there is so little chance that I can ever bear them. My darling, I ache with the loss of the things I cannot give you."* If I had said these things aloud, they would have sounded maudlin, and I could not. He had shown he knew and understood, and that was enough.

A few days later, Jim came bearing triumphantly a small paper-bound volume, which he gave to me. On the cover was a bold inscription:

WHAT I HAVE LEARNED ABOUT WOMEN
by
James Anderson Huff, Jr.

"This ought to be impressive," I commented as I opened it. Inside there was nothing but blank paper.

In my usual indelicate fashion, I held my nose, to Jim's vast delight. He pretended to be on the defensive so he could elaborate on his subject. "The longer I live with you," he said, "the less I know about women, so I had it all put in one volume."

By this time we knew that we were never to have children of our own. Many of our childless friends had adopted children, and after I got out of the hospital, Jim and I began to discuss this possibility. Finally, we decided to try it. We went to Nashville to the Children's Home and made an application. For a while nothing happened.

One day in March Jim sent Bob McGhee, who was both friend and Jim's "Man Friday," out to the farm for me. When I saw his old truck rattling up the road, I wondered why he was coming.

He got out of the truck, grinning happily. "Miss Jane, Mr.

Huff said you got a call from the Children's Home in Memphis. He wants you to come to town and take the call with him."

I hadn't really dared to hope before—but now I didn't just *hope*, I *knew* they had a child for us. They wouldn't have called long distance for any other reason. My guess was right. They had a three-and-a-half-year-old boy for us to see. We were so pleased that we set out at once.

Mrs. Elrod met us at the Home and introduced us to the matron, Miss Tann. They spent some time giving us details of his background—while I waited impatiently just to *see* him. I was relieved when Miss Tann led us into the sitting room to meet him.

Yesterday at this time, I hadn't even known he existed. Now it seemed I had been waiting forever to see this sturdy child in short blue pants and a blue cotton shirt. He had rosy cheeks and a fair skin, his brown hair had just been wet and combed carefully back, and his wide, bright-blue eyes were fringed with long black lashes. At the moment, he was almost overwhelmed with the four adults in the room. Miss Tann and Mrs. Elrod realized this and excused themselves. "You see, son?" said Miss Tann as she left, "I told you we'd find you a mother and daddy."

Children always gravitated to Jim, and in less time than it takes to tell, the boy was in Jim's lap, talking a mile a minute with almost breathless excitement. Jim soon included me in the conversation. He was too shy to say much to me—and I hadn't the faintest idea what to say to him. But Jim and I looked at each other over his head. We wanted him.

When Miss Tann came back, she asked what we were going to call him. We hadn't discussed it, but now Jim answered without hesitation. "John," he said.

There were then just a few formalities, and John was ours. We thanked the matron, said our goodbyes, and went to the car to start the journey home.

When we stopped that night at a motel, John and I went into the room together while Jim stopped at the office. I started to open our suitcases, then I glanced at John. He was staring at me, and said in a tone of both awe and pleasure, "Mama, you're pretty!" Needless to say, from then on we hit it off very well.

John was thrilled with everything. He loved the station wagon and rode in majesty on the high third seat. He loved the farm, and the little red wagon Jim bought for him.

Jim had infinite patience in working with John—and there was very much to teach him. He had never done many of the simplest things which children do: he had not the vaguest idea how to turn a somersault—and Jim and I taught him with much hilarity, both of us doing it for him to see! Jim brought him a tricycle and taught him to ride it. Jim also had some idea of letting John help him in the garden, but John flayed about so wildly that every living thing within his reach was flattened to the ground. Jim wisely found a place for him to dig alone, where he could harm nothing, in the middle of the peach orchard. There he spent hours on end with a shovel, digging enormous holes.

John was delighted with the pigs and chickens. He liked to scatter corn for them to eat—he liked the noise and excitement as they came running to him. And how he loved to gather eggs! Unfortunately, he tended to clutch the eggs a little too tightly when he gathered them, to clunk one upon the other in the basket until I persuaded him that gathering eggs was woman's work, and not for men.

Some dreams refuse to be banished. Every practical consideration may be against them; they may seem buried and long forgotten. But in some far corner of the mind they linger unnoticed, ready to come forth again when conditions are right.

It was in 1947 that Jim had had his short-lived dream of entering the ministry. We had both recognized it as being a little quixotic—and more than a little late. And yet, and yet . . . our dreams *do* shape our destiny, if they come from the heart, for they determine our choices. We may never achieve our dreams, but we are inevitably drawn toward them. There was something in both of us which had responded to that dream of Jim's. We both wished in our hearts it were possible to make it a reality.

For some time Jim and Woods had wanted to reorganize the mills, but could not because of problems existing before their time. The original offer to buy the mills had seemed providential, a solution which would benefit the stockholders and still keep the town's economy stable. When the sale fell through, they continued as before.

Their problems, however, remained. In the late spring of 1951, Jim came home to talk to me about it. "Jane," he said, "Woods and I have decided there is no reasonable solution to our problems at the mill. We've tried every legal way to handle the situation—even talked over a few illegal ones, but nothing is really practical. If we could sell as a going concern, the reorganization would be automatic. We've been checking on possibilities, and we'll probably go to New York and to Chicago next week to see what can be done."

Again I asked the inevitable question: "Jim, if the mills are sold, what will you do?"

He shrugged. "Oh, Jane," he said, "I'm not altogether sure. I wanted so much to go into the ministry when we talked about this before. I still do. When the way was closed then, it seemed God didn't intend for me to be a minister. This year, though, it has become more and more evident to me that men are hungering for the Word of God, and perhaps I could do more good spending the rest of my life giving men this message than in any other way."

"Well, why don't you talk to Hugh about it?" I asked. Hugh Simon was our new, young minister, and a close friend.

Hugh liked the idea. "You know," he said, "you could ask Presbytery to take you under its care, with a view to licensing you after you take one year of seminary work, then ordaining you after your second year. I would recommend that you forget about college—we could take your experience and service in place of college work. You could go directly to seminary as a special student, taking just two years of work instead of the full course for a degree. It's the kind of thing which isn't often done—but I believe that everyone in the Presbytery would agree that you're an exceptional case. Taking years out to finish college would shorten your time of usefulness. Do you want me to put it up to Presbytery?"

It was a gracious and tempting offer, but Jim did not feel that he could accept. The question of selling the mill was still completely unsettled, and Jim could not consider leaving any responsibility, no matter how much he might want to.

Late in July, Jim and I were working in our garden patch on top of the hill. Jim was hoeing around his precious tomatoes. This was the third year we had worked the little vegetable patch behind the house. Set on top of the hill, we had a magnificent view—but never enough water. Jim had worked patiently with it, though, watered and sprayed and tended it, and after two years of scrubby return, it was beginning to produce a little more generously.

Jim hoed the earth around each plant, and staked and tied them. "If I ever do get to seminary," he said, "remind me to write a sermon on tomatoes. It occurs to me that a man raising tomatoes is like a Christian tending to the needs of his soul."

I realized how much Jim wanted to go to seminary. I didn't want to sway him—yet I wanted with all my heart to see him do it. I rather wished Hugh would speak to him again.

That night we were at prayer meeting. The session of the church met once a month after this service, and Jim went back to the study for it. I lingered on purpose in the church, hoping to have a chance to speak to Hugh. "Good night, Jane," he said cheerily as we met in the aisle.

All the other worshipers had left the sanctuary, and though I knew the session members were waiting in the study for Hugh, it might be some time before I had another good opportunity to speak to him. "Hugh," I said, "Jim keeps going back to this idea of entering the ministry. But something keeps pulling him back. I don't know if it's worry over me or what, but I wish you'd try to find out. I want him to do it, but I think it would be wrong for me to say so."

Hugh looked at me in surprise. "I shouldn't think *you* would want him to go!"

His surprise implied that I would have to give up every bit as much as Jim would, and that I might not be willing or capable of doing so. There was no time to argue the point; the men were waiting for him. "I understand all that's involved," I said, "and with all my heart I want him to go. I just don't want to influence his decision."

Hugh smiled at me, then said warmly, "I hope he decides to do the right thing." He passed on into the study.

Almost two weeks later the decision came. It was one of those surprisingly cool August mornings which remind you that summer won't last much longer. John had wakened us at half-past-five, which never bothered Jim, even if it did me.

"Come on, Jane," he said. "We're awake—let's get up. I've a heavy day ahead of me, and I can get my dictation done before anyone comes into the office if I get away early."

I made a face at him and got up. His diet had long since become routine, so I prepared and measured his breakfast almost automatically, then prepared a simpler and less involved breakfast for John, myself, and my sister's little daughter, who was staying with us at the time. I got it all on the table just as the three of them seated themselves to have our Bible reading and prayer.

Jim had opened his mouth to read when his eyes were caught by a movement outside the window. "Be still and look," he cautioned softly.

We looked. About sixty feet from the plate-glass window, a pair of red foxes were marching proudly across the lawn, lifting their paws high and setting them down carefully in the dew-drenched grass, their great plumed tails held haughtily erect. They looked somehow like a pair of arrogant dowagers bearing parasols to an afternoon tea. We watched spellbound as they daintily picked their way across the lawn and disappeared into the woods.

It was a breathtaking moment. The rising sun had gilded the trees and struck fire to the clouds, making a field of diamonds of the heavily dewed grass. The river wound serenely southward into the distance, and the lush green of a rainy summer clothed the hills and valleys. Across this magnificent scene had come the foxes, as silently as in a dream. It was almost too beautiful to be borne.

When we turned back at last to Jim, it seemed natural that instead of reading, he should bow his head in prayer. Spontaneously, the children bowed their heads too. "God, for all the beauty we see around us, and for eyes to see it, we thank You. Help us to open our hearts and lives outward that we may share Your beauty with others. Amen."

Then he began the reading. This morning it was from the twelfth chapter of Romans: "I beseech you, therefore, brethren, by the mercies of God, that ye present your bodies a living sacrifice, holy, acceptable unto God, which is your reasonable service. And be not conformed to this world: but be ye transformed by the renewing of your mind, that ye may prove what is that good, and acceptable, and perfect will of God. . . ." We both knew the words by heart, and I, for one, could never hear them unmoved.

Suddenly, Jim stopped reading and looked across the table at me, his gaze as compelling as a touch. "Jane," he said, "I have to go. I am too old to think about it—but I must go anyhow, no matter what it costs. I'll make some suitable arrangement about the mill, and God willing, I'll go on to seminary next semester." He reached across the table and took my hand. "It means we'll have to leave this, you know. Is it too much to ask of you? You wanted this house so much—are you going to mind leaving it?"

"I suppose I wanted the house *too* much," I admitted. "I've loved it, Jim, but I've been hoping and praying these last weeks that the ministry would be your choice. I've wanted that more than I've wanted the house. I've had my house; now I'll be content to leave it and go wherever you are called to go."

I was really a little surprised that I was so very exultant, for I had loved my house more than any place I had ever been. But I loved my husband more, and if his mission was to go out to preach, nothing so small as a house could be allowed to hinder him. After all, "home is where the heart is," and our home would be wherever Jim was.

When Jim came home for supper a few days later, I knew he had good news he was just bursting to tell, but which he was going to dangle before me until he had gotten the last bit of fun and suspense out of it. He came through the door in the dancing, light-footed way he had when he was happy, and walked me almost all the way around the room.

"Jane," he said jubilantly at last, "we've sold the mills! All of them! It's a package deal, and they're going to keep them running. I'm free to go! Besides, it was a terrific sale. We got our asking price. Woods and I would have been willing to let it go for less if we'd had to."

There now remained only formal application to Presbytery and seminary, and the job of telling Jim's family and friends. It would all have to move without a hitch, as less than two weeks remained before the opening of the seminary term.

Jim went early the next day to tell his mother of his decision. I really dreaded going, for I was afraid she wouldn't approve. Although Jim and I had been talking about this for some time, we hadn't mentioned it to his family—and we weren't sure how they would take it.

I finally steeled myself to pay Jim's mother a visit, just after he had given her the news. "Jim came in a while ago to tell me he is going to seminary so he can enter the ministry," she announced. "Is that what you want him to do, Jane?"

"Yes, I do."

"Good. I see now it is what he should have done twenty-five years ago—only I think I wouldn't have wanted him to do it then."

Until she said that, I hadn't realized how tense I had been. I had been braced for an argument—but there was a warm and gentle pride in her voice which set me at ease. She approved. She wanted him to do it. It was so good to know he was to go with her blessing. I was deeply grateful to her in that moment, and realized I had grown to love her very much.

All at once there was much to say, but I found myself too shy to say it, too afraid to sound "maudlin" as she would have said. I bent over to kiss her cheek and went downstairs.

On the twenty-third of August, Jim wrote to Presbytery asking that he be taken under their care as a candidate for the ministry. His situation was unusual. Presbytery was the governing body of the local churches, and was made up of the minister and one ruling elder from every church in its jurisdiction. Jim had been a ruling elder for ten years, and the elder most often representing his church at Presbytery. He had served as moderator of the Presbytery and had represented the Presbytery at its General Assembly, the highest governing body of the church. He was at this time also a trustee of the Chattanooga Presbytery, and secretary of the Presbyterian Men's Council in the Synod of the Mid-South. He had served on the committee for the examination and licensing of candidates—and now he appealed to them to receive him as a candidate himself.

His application had first to be endorsed by his own session —and as he was the clerk of the session, he had to resign so someone else could write the letter endorsing him. Our good friend Zirkle Cooper was elected pro tem, and after the session's action wrote a warm and gracious letter to Presbytery. All this was done on Wednesday night.

On Thursday, Hugh Simon took Jim's request and the session's endorsement to Atlanta, where Presbytery was meeting. "There was a great deal of enthusiasm," Hugh reported. "Quite a number of the men present got up and spoke on your behalf, Jim. They agreed to waive the requirement for a Bachelor's degree, in view of your long service and wide experience, and will make that recommendation to the seminary."

The die was cast. Jim was going to be a minister. I was caught in a wave of enthusiasm for this new career. True, we must leave this place I loved so well. I would miss the view, the purple valleys, the hills of home. We had had so much here. It could have been all that was needed, but Jim had "desired the higher gifts, seen the more excellent way." Once he felt that God had definitely meant for him to be a minister, he could never again be satisfied with life as it had been.

It could have been so easy and safe and staid—except for that "divine discontent," this dream which was folly by the world's standards. But isn't this what distinguishes man from the other creatures, the ability to "dream dreams, see visions," and to set out on an unknown way in answer to them? It is the upward call which draws man out of himself. Some must go, for "Where there is no vision, the people perish."

BOOK II

THE HOUSE
OF THE LORD

*". . . my cup runneth over. Surely goodness and mercy
shall follow me all the days of my life:
and I will dwell in the house of the Lord for ever."*

PSALMS 23:5–6

Chapter 7

ONCE JIM knew surely that he could go to seminary, he felt a tremendous sense of urgency. "Let's go to Louisville," he said, "to see the Presbyterian seminary there. There's so little time before school starts. I can't afford to lose another year."

"Why Louisville?" I asked.

"I like their program. The Louisville men have shown up well in the Presbytery examinations for licensing and ordination, and they seem to have their feet on the ground, with real love and concern for people. I'm interested in their field-work program, too."

"What's that?"

"Well, every man there does real work in a church while he is in seminary. I like that idea. I don't want to lose touch with things for two years while I study. I need the study, but I want to be working with people at the same time."

Some weeks before, Jim had made preliminary inquiries to several seminaries and had sent for transcripts of his college credits. These he took with him to Louisville on a stifling August day. At the seminary we met the president, Dr. Frank Caldwell, a tall, distinguished-looking man, with a thick handsome shock of white hair.

"I've looked forward to meeting you, Mr. Huff," he said. "I've had some remarkable recommendations of you from the Chattanooga Presbytery, and I think you are to be com-

79

mended for your ambition to enter the ministry at your age. But you didn't send us a transcript of your college record," he added a little sternly. "It's necessary even though you intend to enter as a special student."

I had never seen Jim look so discomfited. "I just didn't dare *mail* a transcript to you," he said sheepishly. "I didn't spend much time studying while I was at the University of Virginia. I'm afraid I spent more time in New York and Washington than I did on campus. But that was twenty-five years ago. I believe you'll find my ideas of studying have changed a bit since."

I could almost see Dr. Caldwell's lips pucker as he looked at the transcript, but he didn't whistle openly. "I see what you mean," he said. "But from the letters we've received about you, I would say *you* have changed a bit, too. Of course, we couldn't accept you as a student here if these were last year's grades, but I believe we can make allowances for all the accomplishments in between. You realize, though, that it isn't going to be easy to begin studying again at the graduate-school level. It's hard work for most of the men who come here directly from college with all their study habits intact."

"I know," Jim said, "it will take tremendous self-discipline to keep up with the work. I've really thought very seriously of going back to take the additional college work to prepare myself, yet I have such a feeling that there's really no time to be lost, that I feel I must go on without it if you think you can take me in spite of my college record. . . ."

"Frankly, it isn't the sort of thing we often do. We've had older men as students before—and often they have just 'fizzled out.' Still, you seem to have a very clear call, and you've been very highly recommended. We need more ministers with your depth and background. I'd like to see you do it."

I received my first powerful impression of the spirit of the seminary at the formal opening service, with the first line of the first hymn. After years of predominantly female congregations in average churches, where the singing is often carried by a few while the rest timidly mouth the words, this singing was a delight and a revelation. This congregation was made up largely of men, and there wasn't a timid voice among them. They had taken quite literally the admonition to "Make a joyful noise to the Lord," and were doing it in exultant, full-throated harmony which stirred the heart.

At the reception which followed I began to meet students and faculty. Jim had been in Louisville only a few days, and seminary activities had just begun—yet as we threaded our way through the crowded social hall, Jim introduced me to one person after another.

I had met Dr. Caldwell before seminary opened. Now Jim introduced me to Mrs. Caldwell, who in her cheerful charming way was making everyone feel welcome. We met Ernie and Betty Smith—"You'll be seeing more of them," Jim said. "Ernie is president of the Student Body, and Betty is president of the Divinity Dames. Now I want you to meet Jim Thorn here, and this is John D. Reese."

So it went. Jim introduced me to forty or fifty people he already knew. I could make only a few of the names stick in my mind—but Jim with his fantastic memory and intense interest in people remembered them all.

Toward the beginning of the second week of seminary, the office passed out a list of all the students enrolled. I came across one of these among Jim's things. Most of the names were already neatly checked—and there was a note on the top of the first page, "forty-three men I do not know." I never mentioned it—it would have embarrassed him to be caught being so methodical. But I knew it wouldn't be long before he would know each of those forty-three men, too.

Our first problem when Jim entered the seminary was finding a place to live. My mother and niece were staying with us, and we had to have a fairly large apartment to accommodate them as well as ourselves and John. Dr. Caldwell sent us to the seminary's housing office, but their listings were for small apartments with only one bedroom. They referred us to several real estate agents, with the assurance that one of them would surely come up with something.

However, there was just very little available for rent. What we saw was either too small, or too unpromising to live in for two years. We drove up one street and down another. At last, we decided we would have to *buy* a house. This turned out to be as discouraging as hunting a place to rent.

Several times in our wanderings, we passed an attractive brick apartment house with a "For Sale" sign on the front. It was old but well built, and on a very pleasant street. I couldn't put it out of my mind.

When I asked the agent about it, she said at once that we wouldn't be interested. However, as nothing else had turned up and seminary was to begin in a week, I asked if we might see it. It was far more expensive than anything we had dreamed of, but it was perfect for us. The apartments were enormous—three and four bedrooms, large, high-ceilinged rooms—and the property brought in a good income. Since Jim had sold his mill stock the week before, we were temporarily prosperous. We decided it would make a good solid investment.

Long afterward, Dr. Caldwell mentioned this incident to me. His eyes sparkled as he told me how astonished he had been at our solution to the housing problem. "Maybe at the time you weren't aware of the usual finances of seminary students—but I assure you it was the first time in the history of Louisville Presbyterian Seminary that a student had bought an apartment house to live in while studying."

Actually, Jim *did* fully realize the difference between his own financial situation and that of many of his fellow students. It was to trouble him all the time he was there. This was not a new situation, but it was painfully obvious here, and buying the apartment house unfortunately helped to make it more so. Jim and I had both long been aware—and deeply concerned —about the privations of most of those in the ministry. In these first months of seminary, though, it was driven home to us as never before.

The seminary itself was not too well endowed—although in appearance it was handsome and well kept. Dr. Caldwell once spoke to me about the difficulty of raising funds for seminaries. "The dollar for seminary education is the hardest of all to obtain," he said. "People see the need for orphanages, for missions, for colleges, but for leadership, for the training that is so essential to keep our churches going—there is not enough money given. It is heartbreaking to tell a willing man there is not room for him, or money enough to keep him going through the year."

Except for Jim, every student in the seminary was a college graduate, for Presbyterians believe in an educated ministry. In this age of high salaries and unusual demand for trained people, most of them would have been well rewarded for their education and ability in business. But they hadn't chosen an easy or lucrative path. The sacrifices these men were making were complicated by the fact that most of them were married. Many even had children.

Once the seminary frowned upon the admission of married students and recommended that they leave their families while they studied! But times change; by the time we went to Louisville, the situation was almost reversed. By senior year, in fact, there were seldom more than four single men in a class.

There was still controversy over whether or not it was advisable for students to marry before coming to seminary. The fact remains that many of them do, and I for one, think it a good custom. In no other vocation can a wife normally share to the same degree her husband's work. In most vocations, a man's family and his business are things apart; in the ministry, this is not so. What a minister's wife is and what she does before the world is in some ways even more eloquent testimony than any word he can say. She can be a source of comfort and strength to him and an inspiration to his flock or she can belittle her husband's ministry with every word and action, as if to tell the world that his witness in his own home has so little worth that she cannot follow after him.

The seminary, however, was never intended to accommodate families, so there was a good deal of crowding. Dormitories designed only for the use of single men weren't exactly comfortable as family accommodations.

The situation of the students who lived off-campus was often far worse. Many of them served rural areas, and the time and expense of getting to and from the seminary was a real drain. Some had to leave their families and live in a dormitory during the week. This was very hard on their wives, and they would always feel divided in loyalties and emotions. And all too often, there just wasn't money enough to make ends meet.

We were at this time far from wealthy, and had to budget our resources very carefully to support us while Jim was at the seminary and over the lean years we knew were to come. But since so many of the other students were in real want, and since Jim's background was widely known, we gave the appearance of opulence, whatever the reality.

Jim's background was the subject of numerous student jokes, just about all of them good natured I am happy to say. He still had many business connections and continued to receive a rather heavy mail. Most of his business correspondence was sent to the seminary. He often picked it up between classes, and went through it quickly while waiting for his next class to begin. It became a standard joke that he was shuffling through all his stocks and bonds. But Jim's good sense and good humor, plus his truly loving and generous nature soon won him the affection and respect of his classmates.

As a matter of fact, his background and experience gave him a breadth of viewpoint which impressed many of them deeply. There was a time when most ministers didn't know anything about business or business administration and were proud of it. There had been a time when in popular thought a capitalist had to be evil. Public opinion, always on a pendulum, has now begun to swing back to middle ground. There has come a feeling that a man *can* have practical knowledge and still maintain his moral principles.

Because, however, wealth has often come by avarice, there is still a tendency among idealists to favor the side of labor over management in any and all cases. I was told of a visitor lecturing on labor relations. He took the position that since labor works with its hands, it deserves all it can get. "The man was a persuasive speaker," I was told, "and we were all in agreement with every word he said, until Jim brought us all up short. He quietly asked, 'Doctor, have you ever risked all you had to buy machinery and materials, then undertaken to meet a regular payroll to men who just operate that machinery, paying regular salaries through times of loss as well as times of profit?' "

"It was such a simple question," said the classmate who told me this story, "but none of us had ever thought of it just that way before. Once we had, we realized that the businessman has some problems of his own. I think all of us who were there will be more likely to broaden our views of the relations between capital and labor in the future."

One of Jim's most endearing qualities was his ability to laugh at himself. He would often preface a classroom recitation with, "Of course, I don't have a college education like the rest of you fellows," said in an artless tone which always delighted his classmates.

Jim had a marked influence on a number of his fellow students, from his first weeks at seminary. Here his greater age and experience worked to his advantage. People always gravitated toward him, but his relations with these younger men were particularly marked by affection and respect.

I recall especially a charming and obviously lonely young man whom we met and invited out to dinner. I was very much impressed by his intelligence and wit, but there was something about him that bothered me.

I couldn't resist quizzing Jim about him.

"What do you think of him?" I asked.

"What do you mean?"

"Well, I know you're not supposed to make snap judgments. But, Jim, I kept thinking he was one of the most attractive young men I had ever seen, that he was going to take honors at seminary, and then trot out into the biggest and richest church he could find and be lionized by the ladies."

Jim laughed at me. "What a terrible thing to say!" he scoffed. "That may be just what he's planning *now*—but give him time and give God time. Three years in seminary will do a lot for him."

I don't know whether or not this chance conversation had anything to do with it—but Jim singled out this young man. For the next three years he was a frequent visitor in our home, and remained a close and dear friend to us both.

Several years later, when he was the beloved pastor of a church in a small Southern town, we were doing a bit of reminiscing. "I'll never forget the first time I came to your house," he said. "You had cooked turkey and fried ham, and I was so hungry for home-cooked food, it seemed to me the best thing I had ever tasted in my life. And the laughter and fellowship around your table were more fun than any I had ever known. . . ."

One confidence led to another. I couldn't resist telling him about my obviously mistaken first impression of him. But I soon thought I had done something terribly wrong, that I had overstepped the limits of friendship. His face froze in amazement and shock. *"Me and my big mouth,"* I thought, *"I've put my foot in it again."*

"But, Jane," he said in astonishment, "that is just exactly what I was when I met you and Jim. I had lived all my life with people who were richer than I, and somehow I had gotten the notion that the most important thing in the world was to be rich. Then I felt I was called to the ministry, but I didn't want to be a minister. I fought it just as long as I could, but always I had the sure sense that God called me. Finally, when I simply *had* to go, I had one last defiant word for God: *'All right,'* I thought, *'I'll be a minister, but somehow I'm going to be a rich one!'*

"I don't think that there was anything at seminary that could have changed me. It just wasn't something they were equipped to handle—but Jim Huff was. You couldn't live long around him without realizing that God came first, people came next, and it didn't really matter if riches never came at all. There was something about Jim and his way of living that put my life into a proper perspective. By the time I was ordained, I was quite willing to go wherever God called me, to whatever task.

"I am where I am today because of Jim. I'll never be rich by the world's standards, but I'm rich in ways I never dreamed of when I went so reluctantly to seminary. In a way God let me keep my boast, but He made it better than anything I could have planned."

Despite his maturity and experience, there were some very real problems for Jim. He was completely out of practice in academic work, and knew none of the tricks of the trade. Perhaps the most arduous discipline of all was that of writing papers. I came into our room late one night to find him working at the typewriter in a positive agony of concentration. "What on earth are you working at?" I asked.

"I'm trying to do a term paper," he said. "I don't believe I've ever done one before."

"But where are your notes?"

"I don't have any. I've done all my studying, and I have it all organized in my head. That's the way I always did all my business correspondence."

"Well, organizing it all in your head will be just fine when you get into preaching," I warned, "but you've got to make notes to write papers. You get some three-by-five-inch note cards, then take notes on everything you read that pertains to what you intend to write about—then you can quote accurately—and give credit where credit is due!"

Jim dutifully came home the next day with five thousand note cards. "Jim," I wailed, "did you have to buy all they had?"

He grinned amiably at me. "Guess I'll be using them a few years. It occurred to me that they'll be just the right size to make sermon notes on, so I figured I might as well get enough to hold me."

In the course of a few weeks, our life was completely changed. Jim had become so absorbed in what he was doing that there was simply no time for the wide range of interests he had enjoyed before he came to seminary. The golf clubs gathered dust in the closet, the chessmen lay idle in their cases, and the beloved cameras lay unused. It was the limitation of hours, the limits of a man who could do just so much in twenty-four hours. At least, I thought, once mid-term tests were over, he could take a breather. It didn't work out that way.

He looked worn out when he came in after the tests were over. "Jim, what's wrong?" I asked. "You look bad."

"I don't know," he said wearily. "I think I'd better see the doctor."

I left him at the doctor's office and an hour later he phoned. "Jane, I've got to go to the hospital. I'm evidently way out of control. Can you pack a bag for me and come take me out there?"

As I hung up the phone, I felt very guilty. How had we been so complacent? We should have seen a doctor as soon as we got to Louisville, but Jim's vital personality and unfaltering determination to keep on going made it so easy to forget that he was diabetic. We hadn't stopped to realize that with all the strenuous exercise of past years ended now for lack of time, Jim's diet and insulin intake had to be reconsidered.

At the hospital he was once again something of a medical curiosity. Almost anyone else with as much sugar in his blood would have been in a coma; Jim had been taking tests in graduate school.

"Did you say you'd taken some tests just before you came?" the doctor asked.

When Jim replied he had, the doctor said, "Well, was your thinking clear—or did you just think it was?"

Jim grinned, "Well, I *thought* I was thinking clearly—we'll see when I get out."

He was shocked to find he needed to take his tests over. It was fortunate that the doctor had warned him what to expect. As it was, it took him several days in the hospital, plus a radical change in his diet and insulin intake, to return to normal.

Back in Tennessee, Jim's brother Woods had been busy making plans to leave Rockwood and start a business of his own. Then he learned his mother had cancer of the spine.

In a family as close and completely devoted to one another as this one, it went without saying that one of her sons must remain at home during the long and painful ordeal ahead. Jim was already gone. Without even consulting him, Woods canceled his own plans and assumed the burden at home. "In brotherly love, preferring one another. . . ." He did not even telephone, but wrote Jim the news of their mother's illness and his own decision.

Jim silently handed the letter to me. As I read it, I realized that his mother had been ill in those last few days before we had left for Kentucky and hadn't wanted us to know. But should Jim go back? Was this, on top of the great difficulty Jim had already encountered in studying and the physical handicap of his diabetes, an indication that Jim really should give up and go home? "Should you go, Jim?" I asked.

Perhaps he sensed the implication behind my question, perhaps there was some temptation in the suggestion. "I've set my course, Jane," he replied firmly. "There is no turning back now. Somehow I don't really have a choice—I am here, and Woods is at home, and that is the way of it."

Chapter 8

NOT LONG after he was out of the hospital, Jim came home to report that Dr. Hanna, the director of field work, had asked him to serve as student pastor to two small churches in Indiana.

"That sounds like a big job," I said. I couldn't help but show my concern. "What did you tell him?"

"What do you think I told him? I said I'd go Sunday to preach and let them look me over. If they like me, and I like them, we'll take them on." With Jim, it was always "we." I was happy to be consulted—even if only afterward.

"Jim, I wish you wouldn't take a church now," I protested. "It seems to me you have all you can do already."

"Jane, I'm going to do what I'm asked to do," he said patiently. "I'm not going to have exceptions made for me—if I need to, then I haven't any business here. I came to Louisville because of the field work—because I knew I could continue to work with people in a church right through seminary—and that's what I'm going to do."

"Well, you came as a special student," I argued, "and you aren't working for a degree. I don't care if you look thirty-three —you're forty-four, and you aren't as young as you think you are!" Even as I talked, I knew it was useless. No limitation of age or health would stop him. He *couldn't* take the easy way out.

Jim took me with him that first Sunday. We got an early start, for he was always a stickler for punctuality. The two

91

churches were twelve miles apart, forty miles or so north of
Louisville. The December day was bleak and bitterly cold. "We
go to Sharon Hill for a service at nine-thirty," Jim told me,
"then we drive over to Lexington for a service at eleven o'clock."

Sharon Hill proved to be a small, white frame, country
church set in a clearing in the woods miles from the highway on
a gravel road. Shortly after we got there, other cars began to
arrive. Jim and I introduced ourselves to the congregation as
they came, until Bob Richter, who was then student minister,
arrived with his wife Betty.

The inside of the church was as plain as an old-fashioned
kitchen, and terribly cold. The pews were old, upright, and
unyielding, built by the same hands which had framed the
church, and boxed in at the bottom to keep out drafts. On the
left side of the church, a pot-bellied coal stove took the place
of three pews. Close to it there was an illusion of warmth,
and we huddled nearby for a few minutes, talking, as Betty
introduced me to others coming in. Then one of the women
went to the piano to begin the service. The men moved away
to sit on the right side of the church, and Betty inconspicuously
guided me to a seat on the left. I noticed that even the children
separated in like fashion, the boys sitting with their mothers
only if they were too little to be trusted to sit alone on the men's
side.

Actually, there were few children, and many older people.
Almost without exception, the women were plainly and simply
dressed, with little concession to fashion, in clothes which were
carefully chosen to last. But in spite of the temperature, they
had a warmth that came from the heart, something sincere and
enduring and likeable.

Because of the cold, I think Bob shortened the service, and
Jim didn't preach long. He didn't really seem to be "preaching"
at all, but spoke quietly as if he were talking to a group of his
personal friends. After the service, the elders asked if he would
come again the following Sunday. It was a good start, and I felt
better.

On our way to Lexington, where the Richters were to meet us again, Jim told me what he had learned from them about the area. "It's really a dying farm section," he said. "I don't suppose this land was ever too productive—now it would take real money to make it produce. The younger men and women went away during the war—into the service or well-paid defense jobs. Only one or two have come back to stay and make their homes here. Seems like these congregations are made up mostly of older men and women, and children not yet old enough to leave home."

"What will they be like to work with?"

"Oh, difficult, I imagine. It would take a good year just to win their confidence, before you could really do any work at all. It's been years since they've been able to afford a regular minister—and they've grown used to having student ministers come to supply their pulpits while they learn to preach. They're just barely tolerant of all these fresh young hopes—and tolerance can soon become apathy. I think Bob is pretty well discouraged. He says he can see so many things to be done, but no one wants to change things from the way they've always done them."

"Do you think your 'fresh young enthusiasm' can change them?" I asked to tease him.

"Doubt if I can do much—but don't forget, God can change people. That's what I'm banking on. It'll be interesting to see what happens."

We had driven into the town of Lexington, so small it fitted almost entirely around a central square. On one side was the church, which was about twice as large as the church at Sharon Hill. It was also white frame but bulked large and square against the sky.

Despite the size of the church, the congregation here was smaller. The church was heated by a furnace in the basement, and was a good deal warmer than at Sharon Hill, but there was an indefinable difference in the atmosphere. The people were a little better dressed, but more guarded. They sat in several distinct little groups—I guessed there were several "cliques" which could be, as Jim had said, difficult. There were more children, though, who had stayed for the church service after Sunday school.

The service here was a little longer, a little more formal, and though Jim used the same topic, he developed it somewhat differently. I sensed a demanding attitude, covert rather than expressed, which I found myself resenting just a little.

After church we met many of the people, and the first general impression was dispelled in the warm greetings we received from individuals.

I was especially struck by the Renschlers—they were such a big, handsome, outgoing tribe. Dale Renschler was massive in build, tall and powerful, a man who obviously liked to be out of doors and busy with his hands. His wife seemed slight beside him. She taught in the high school in Scottsburg, not because her family had any need of money, for Dale was obviously successful, but because the work satisfied her. In introducing his children, Dale had the sort of proud, yet awed humility of a man who has never gotten over a miracle—and there was some justification for his feelings in the bright, alert faces of his daughter and two sons.

I was introduced all around while Bob and Jim met with the elders. The Richters then took us to the ancient manse which was provided for the minister of the two churches.

It was a tall, two-story salt box of soft native brick, perhaps a hundred years old. There were two rooms on each floor, divided by a wide hall and the stairs. In the rear, a dining room and kitchen had been added, and much later, a bath had also been tacked on. The house was large and plain, and had a certain dignity—but there was no practical way of heating it through the long, hard Ohio Valley winter.

"We leave one heater—in the kitchen—going all winter," Betty told us. "Then, as soon as we come in from Louisville on Friday night, we light the big oil heater—it warms the living and dining rooms. We have to live only in these three rooms. When it's cold, we don't go upstairs at all, just sleep in the living room."

"What they really need here," said Bob, "is a small, compact manse. It's cold here for so much of the year that this big old house is impossible. But with a new manse, they could attract a full-time ordained minister."

"How do the people of the church feel about building a new manse?" asked Jim.

"Some, like Dale Renschler, are very enthusiastic. Others feel 'there's no sense in indulging these young ministers in all these new-fangled notions.' " He pursed his lips and spoke in a tone of sharp disapproval. We all laughed.

"Then, you've got divided opinions," Jim said drily, "on the wisdom of building?"

"Yes, I'm afraid so. Yet I believe there really is a majority in favor of it. It's a strange group of people. You never truly know what they're thinking. You just have to feel your way along—and pray for guidance."

The Richters spent some time in explaining to us how to keep from freezing to death in the manse. "Why, you don't know yet whether or not they want me," said Jim.

Bob laughed. "They'll want you," he said shortly, "so the problems are all yours. I just have three weeks left here."

As Bob had predicted, both churches voted unanimously the following Sunday to ask Jim to serve as student pastor for the rest of his time at the seminary. So began our "double life." Or perhaps it was really a triple life—for our weeks were divided between Louisville, Lexington, and Sharon Hill. All our work was directed toward the single goal of serving God, yet each area was so different and challenging in its demands that we could greedily wish for all of the time for each of them.

Each Friday in Louisville I packed what groceries and clothes I thought John, Jim, and I would need for the weekend. As soon as John was out of school we went to the seminary to

wait for Jim. When he came out to slip behind the wheel, John
bouncing up and down with excitement, would shout, "Daddy,
Daddy! Let's go. We've been waiting a hundred hours." And
off we went, through Louisville across the Ohio River into
Jeffersonville, Indiana, then out onto the open road.

Once we left the traffic behind us Jim usually began to sing.
His voice was so rich and full of a contagious enthusiasm
that John and I always joined in without waiting to be invited,
and the forty miles rolled away behind us.

When we did not sing, we talked. These drives were oases
of companionship in our too busy days. As always, Jim and I
talked about everything, but especially about our responsibilities and opportunities in the two little Indiana churches. These
people were now our people, even in a sense our family, and we
loved them. We shared their lives, their burdens, and their joys,
and tried to share with them our faith.

This was what the seminary experience was designed to prepare Jim for—but the fullness of his own religious experience,
the maturity of his own spirit had already largely prepared him.
It was no wonder that we went eagerly each weekend to that
barren strip of Indiana which was "ours" in a special sense.

It was slow, slow work—and we had so very little time, for
the church work was just supposed to occupy weekends while
Jim was engaged in a full course of graduate study (we later
figured he had averaged reading a thousand pages a week during this time). The study ought to have come first, as preparation for the years of service ahead. But the heart is not governed
by "ought"—and here the need was so great. When the flock
is small, the good shepherd knows every sheep by name, and
with time, he comes to know every spot and blemish, as well
as every virtue, of the sheep he loves.

Jim could look into the heart of a soldier home from the war
and see the haunting shadows there. He saw the pain of a farmer
who made life a hell for all those who loved him, but most of

all for himself. He saw the shell of self-doubt and distrust which imprisoned a timid housewife, the wall of thorns which a lonely woman raised around her with her sharp and venomous tongue. He saw also the quiet courage and fortitude with which one woman nursed her invalid husband, the love with which a large family surrounded the only daughter, a sweet and loving child of eight, who had only a few short months to live.

Christianity doesn't offer any ready solutions to all the problems of life, nor does it ever offer immunity to them. Christianity is not even primarily concerned with the teaching of morality, or goodness, or self-sacrifice, though these things and many others will very probably follow deep religious conviction. The primary concern of Christianity, and therefore of the minister, is far more than these things, and far more difficult: it is to bring about in the life of every individual a personal encounter with God, an encounter so vivid and so real, that the individual forgets the limitations of self and becomes dedicated to God's service.

All the many facets of the minister's job are directed at this one aim. For Jim, the most natural beginning was through simple neighborliness. He called on his own church members, and on their neighbors—there was soon no one in either community whom he didn't know.

There were small ways in which I could help, and Jim was quick to point them out to me: "Jane, to be of any use to people here, we have to care about them. You only really care about those you know. You have to go among them, see what they are doing, what they are facing, how they are thinking. You have to reach them just where they are before they can begin to realize we haven't come to preach 'at' them, but to share with them."

"Where do you want me to begin?"

"Why don't you go up and see Mrs. Noakes? You'll like her. She is very much isolated because of her husband's stroke, yet she has remained courageous and patient through it all. She'd be ever so pleased if you came—why don't you make one of your good angel food cakes to take along? Milt can't talk yet, but he can eat, and I think he'd enjoy some cake."

One by one, he mentioned homes where he thought I should call. Sometimes his instructions were vague: "She needs a friend, Jane. Just go and sit with her." Sometimes, he had in mind a specific way I could help: "Go as soon as you can, Jane. Her husband is diabetic, and they are finding it such a lot of trouble to keep the hypodermic needles and syringes sterilized that I'm afraid they aren't doing it. You can show her how you do it—you always make it look easy."

I usually went wherever he suggested, and I think I always came away richer than when I went. I made a cake and climbed the hill to see the Noakes. She was a gallant woman, undaunted by the hardships which her husband's long illness had imposed upon her, radiating a sure and quiet faith in God's love and mercy which would see her through whatever she had to endure. I came away deeply moved by her strength and assurance and prayed to God that if ever anything terrible happened to Jim, I would have the strength to be like that.

I went to "sit" with the woman who needed a friend. While neither of us talked very much, I came away refreshed, for I *had* made a friend in the quiet communion we had together.

I went to see the woman whose husband was diabetic, and showed her some of the things I had learned in the hospital in Boston—how to use and care for all the syringes, needles, and sterilizing equipment, and the various methods of testing for sugar. It helped me see my own problems in better perspective.

As Jim had predicted, as I came to know our congregations, I grew to care. One skeptic asked, "Aren't you just nosy? What business is it of yours? You're just supposed to teach religion."

"Oh, it's a very materialistic religion we have," said Jim. "We believe that God is the God of all life, not a heathen idol who waits inside a church building to see who's going to come in on Sunday. To us, there is no divorce between one part of life and another. Jesus was concerned with what people served at their weddings, with the crops, and with the day's catch of fish. He fed the hungry, healed the sick, and gave sight to the blind. And it was out of these concerns of daily life that He drew His teachings of the relationship between God and man. Life was 'all of a piece' to Him, and I see it that way, too."

Lexington drew the greater part of our attention and time. Its membership was larger (though attendance was poorer), so that proportionately it rated more time. Also, because it seemed to be more 'stony ground,' I guess we both were especially zealous in our attempts to cultivate it.

"Jane," Jim said one day as we left the church, "I can't preach the same sermons in those two churches. Do you sense the difference, or is it just my imagination? What is it? Can geography make so much difference?"

"I don't know what it is, Jim," I replied. "I just know there is a difference. I felt it the first time I walked into the Lexington church."

Jim shook his head. "I don't know quite where it lies. Outwardly they are much the same. Both congregations are largely made up of farmers. They are all in much the same economic bracket. . . ."

"Yes," I interrupted, "but there's just something more forthright about Sharon Hill. When they don't like something, they say so. At Lexington, they're never quite with you and they're never quite against you. Do you know what Lexington makes me think of?"

"What?"

"An aging belle, still reciting her triumphs of half a century before, still clinging to her disappointments. It's hard for anyone to think she ever had any real prospects, anyway. I'll bet seventeen people have told me how this used to be the county seat of Scott County, how the county courthouse used to stand on the square where the schoolhouse is now, and how political maneuvering had moved the county seat to Scottsburg. It's like they're still grieving for a lover lost—and the temper of the town has gone sour."

Jim laughed. "Don't judge too quickly," he admonished. "There are a number of people who don't fit into that pattern. There are several who stand staunchly on their own feet, are working to make something of themselves and their town and their churches. Look at Dale Renschler, for instance. He and I have been talking with others about ways to attract some sort of small industry here—maybe something that will make possible piece-work for housewives—some way for them to pick up extra money to improve their homes and farms. There are others who are looking ahead, beyond their own interests."

Perhaps Jim was right, but the work at Sharon Hill was certainly more heart-warming. There were fewer people and even less money, but there was a willingness to work which touched the heart. These people were sympathetic and willing to pitch in, no matter what the cause, whether it was to provide a dinner for the meeting of the parish council, teach in Bible school, or attend a church family night. There was such a loving response to our efforts that it seemed our love was returned fourfold.

It may well be the differences we found in the two churches lay entirely in our own personalities. Perhaps there was no real lack in the people of Lexington but in us. It may have been our failure to lead or inspire which made the difference. In Sharon Hill, we were fortunate that the door was open to us. In Lexington, it never seemed to open more than a crack.

Oddly, it was in Lexington that we were to show the greatest statistical "success," for there was a material gain, an outward show of improvement for the records of Presbytery. But that was only, by Jim's whimsical definition, "paper profit." Neither of us honestly felt that there had been any real spiritual gain. Perhaps there was something we did not see—but which God could measure. If so, it was to be left to another to reap the harvest.

So absorbed had we become in the lives and concerns of our people, that looking back I find it hard to believe that all our time with them was compressed into just a little more than forty-eight hours of each week. We were in Indiana only Friday night, Saturday, and Sunday. During this time, Jim did all his visiting, preached at two morning services, held all church meetings with the elders, deacons, and trustees, served as adult adviser to the evening fellowship of the young people of Sharon Hill, and then drove back immediately afterward to preach at an evening service at Lexington.

Occasionally, when there was a special need, Jim made the trip up during the week. Fortunately, there were not too many unusual demands that first winter: only a few extra meetings, a few cases of illness, and two funerals, both in the Sharon Hill church where the membership was older.

In April Jim interested the elders of the Lexington church in having a special week of services during Holy Week. Instead of preaching himself he invited our former minister, Hugh Simon to come from Rockwood to speak each night during the week. I congratulated Jim on having sense enough not to take on one more job. He smiled at me and commented dryly, "Why, it wasn't that, honey. I just figured they were tired of the sound of my voice, so I thought they deserved a really good speaker for a change."

During the afternoons, Hugh and Jim went visiting, calling on every member of the church during the week, counseling, talking, or just listening.

One evening at supper, Hugh said, "Jim, are you planning to come back to Rockwood when you finish seminary?"

"No," said Jim, "I don't believe you can go back to your home town. 'A prophet is not without honour, save in his own country.' "

Hugh grinned. "I'm glad you've learned that. This afternoon

when we were out calling, I was thinking that it was a whole lot like calling in Rockwood, with just one difference. Here there's a bit of awe, a 'set-apartness' mingled with respect and admiration and love for you. In Rockwood, they think of you with a great deal of love and affection, but there are a lot of people who still talk about you as that Huff boy, even though you're forty-four years old!"

Chapter 9

It was a Thursday afternoon in late April. We were to go to Indiana for the weekend. I was planning a large party for Jim's classmates and friends at seminary the following Tuesday and I was checking off a long list of things which yet remained to be done when the telephone rang. I answered it with no inkling of the happy surprise which lay in store for me.

"Mrs. Huff?"

"Yes."

"This is Mrs. Turner of the Children's Agency. If you are still interested in adopting a child, we have a little girl we would like to tell you about."

"When can we come?"

We had made application to several different agencies in the hope of adopting more children. We wanted another little boy so John would have a companion, but had explained we would be glad to have any child they felt would enjoy our home. "After all," said Jim, "in the normal course of events, you don't get to order a child by age or sex. We'll be delighted to take what comes." Until now, nothing had come, however, despite an exciting flurry of investigation.

At the Children's Agency we learned that "our" little girl (there was never any question about accepting her if we were given the chance) was just eleven months old, as yet spoke only a few words, and had started walking three days before.

"She's still a little unsteady on her feet," said Mrs. Turner, "but she's through with crawling since she tried walking."

We convinced her without difficulty that we wanted the child, and arranged to see her the following day. We were as excited as a pair of nine-year-olds waiting for a birthday party. We had carefully brought up the idea to John—and he was enthusiastic too; he was a gregarious child and desperately wanted company.

When we reached the Children's Agency the next day, our little one was asleep. The nursery was almost too warm, and the heat had flushed her cheeks a delicate pink and curled her short brown hair softly about her head.

We talked in normal voices, for Jim had to go back to seminary and we wanted her to awaken before he left. We all laughed at something Jim had said, and she opened her eyes, looked at him, and smiled. She had awakened in a strange place, and only one of the three of us was at all familiar to her, but she was quite content, and lay beaming at us. Jim spoke quietly to her until, in the most natural way in the world, she put out her arms to be picked up. Mrs. Turner and I exchanged amused glances: Jim might be a Pied Piper with children in general, but this one was going to wrap him around her little finger, and he was going to love it!

We were all for taking her home that day, but Mrs. Turner felt we had better have the weekend to get ready for her. I didn't dare tell her we were expecting over a hundred and fifty guests Tuesday night, for fear she might postpone it further.

Monday morning, before we went down to the Children's Agency, I received an air express package from my sister Martha, containing all the exquisite hand-embroidered clothes which she had made for her daughter Becky. We had phoned to tell her the news Friday night, and she had gotten them all out, washed and ironed them so they looked like new, and shipped them to me. Marie—as we had decided to call her—was well-clothed.

We kept John out of school to go with us, so he could feel he had some part in choosing her. The day was sunny and mild, and the three of us were foolish with excitement. We picked her up, took movies of the occasion, and came home to spend the rest of the day playing with her. She was calm, intelligent, and agreeable to everything.

To my own surprise, by Tuesday night I managed to get the cakes done, the flowers arranged, and though I never finished a slipcover I had foolishly begun, I left it half-pinned together with no apologies. It was a lovely party, and Marie was the belle of the evening.

During the spring quarter, Jim was required to prepare and deliver a sermon in his class on homiletics (the art of preaching). Although, like the other students, Jim was preaching each Sunday in church, it was far more agonizing to preach before sharp-minded, critical classmates and Dr. Caldwell, all of whom were prepared to dissect your sermon, than it was to preach to a group of churchgoers on a Sunday morning.

Jim spent long, earnest hours over the preparation of his sermon. He decided to use the idea that had come to him the year before, on our farm in Rockwood, when he was struggling to raise tomatoes. He labored over it, and then read it to me. It was a homely, touching sermon, full of simple everyday illustrations. Later, when I was beginning to write this book, and made the rounds to talk with those who had known Jim, I found to my astonishment that almost every man in his class remembered that sermon. "It was a simple sermon," one of them recalled, "so simple and so obvious that he seemed almost embarrassed about it. But it has stayed with me through the years."

It *was* a memorable sermon. There was nothing very striking about it, it was as plain and as unpretentious as Jim himself, but behind it lay wisdom and spiritual power which were moving indeed:

A friend of mine gave me advice on growing the best possible tomatoes. "Get yourself a posthole digger," he said, "and dig a hole at least two feet deep. Then mix back into the hole layers of topsoil, then fertilizer,—preferably from the stable. Keep filling your hole until it's within an inch or two of ground level, and leave a depression so plenty of water will be caught. The growing plant will need a great deal of it."

Almost as soon as we put a tiny plant, only two or three inches high, into one of the holes, we drive a stake at least four or five feet tall into the ground beside it. This is done now in preparation for a later need, for after the roots have started growing and spreading, driving in a supporting stake might cut and injure them.

Then begins that part of our work where the hoe becomes an extension for our arms. We must not let any grass or weeds grow up close to our plant to take from it the nourishment which it needs to reach its fullest growth.

As they grow, we take the branches of our vine and bind them firmly to the stake—yet we do it tenderly, so as not to bruise them. We begin also to watch for bugs, and all manner of insects which would eat the leaves and sap the strength of the vine.

Ordinarily, we will use a spray gun, and various recommended sprays against the different types of insects and blight. We must be careful that the nozzle of the spray gun tilts up, so we can spray underneath the leaves, where we cannot always see, and where many of our destroying insects hide. Like most evil, they seem to hide from the heat and light of the sun.

In due season, we come to the point where our vine is grown— full of fruit—and almost ripe for the picking. We, of course, are continuing our never-ending struggle against weeds. If we relax for just a little time, they will take over our garden.

One day we may notice a branch which has fallen from its fastening on the stake. It is touching the earth, and behold: a red, ripe tomato. We stoop excitedly to pick it, but when we do, it squashes in our hand. Almost sick at the rottenness of this, our first fruit, there is nothing for us to do but to throw it "over the hill" into the dump heap. Then we bind that branch up again, hoping that none of the other fruit has been blighted.

Then the fruit begins to ripen on the branches we have tended, and we go out day after day to pick from our vine fruit that is useful and good, fruit which brings us great joy.

The parable of the tending of the garden is so familiar to you that it seems rather foolish to point out the parallel. Still, we do need to have this lesson driven into our hearts, again and again. We are ministers of our Lord and Savior. We are going out to serve Him in gardens that have been prepared and planted for us, in all probability most carefully, and most lovingly, by those who have preceded us in serving in those fields. But we must continue giving to the plants we tend all the food we can, to see that they have a healthy life. So we use our Scriptures to prepare the ground of men's hearts, and our prayers for the Holy Spirit to nourish them.

Perhaps here we need a word of caution: there are times when a plant can be burned up by the application of too much fertilizer, and there are times when we can drive men away from the Lord by the wrong use of the Word. Sometimes we are too eager that *we* should reap the increase of souls for the Kingdom, but there are times when we can only plant, as Paul did, or only water, as Apollos did, and must leave it to God to give the increase. We need to pray continually that we see every opportunity, but also that we do not run before Him in our eagerness.

Remember that stake we drove into the ground? Do you not think it like Christ—something to which we can bind our vines, that they may grow without blemish? Remember how *early* the stake was placed in the ground. In the same way we want to put Christ before our children from their earliest years, that He may be the mainstay and support of their lives. As the stake would cut the roots when they are full-grown, so when Christ enters the heart only in adulthood, part of the individual's life must often be cut off to make room for Him. How easy and how rewarding it is to begin with Christ as a support in early childhood.

We must dig out everything from around our vines that can take away their strength. The only way we can do this is through application to our job—just staying at work with the hoe day after day, trying to remove every temptation we can, helping our people to build good habits rather than bad.

The fertilizer and the spray are like the Word of God. The application of the Word must be continuing, and we must use it wisely as well as liberally. We also need to be continually in study, that we may know the formulae which should be used for each destroyer that we find seeking after our vine.

When we pick the fruit, we must put it to use immediately, if we want to get the best from it. This is one thing we let happen all too often in the church: we pick the fruit, then, rather than put it to use, we set it down for a while and go off in search of others. As we fail to use the first, it spoils. Too many times, a minister has a sense of completion when he has brought a new member into the church, but his job has really just begun. A soul saved is fruit indeed, but it must be put to use in the Kingdom. We must ask ourselves the question, "Saved from sin *to* what?" and help that person find his place of service. Remember that the fruit is also the seed, which in its turn is to grow and bear more fruit. . . .

We are the gardeners of God. We study now to obtain knowledge of tools, of methods, and of materials to use in the Lord's Garden. When we go out into this garden, we accept the responsibility of tending the vines planted in it, and great is our responsibility, for all manner of things are there to spoil the vines. But our Lord has told us, "If ye abide in me, and my words abide in you, ye shall ask what ye will, and it shall be done unto you. Herein is my Father glorified, that ye bear much fruit; so shall ye be my disciples." [St. John 15:7–8]

Believing this, shall we bow our heads together and ask Him for the strength to do our task?

The spring quarter ended at seminary, and we moved to Indiana to spend full time on our two churches. I have always loved the word pastoral—and this was our pastoral summer. Summers in Indiana have a special quality, from the clear bright dawns, through the shimmering heat of noonday, to the awaited coolness of evening. You can feel things growing; the earth has a vibrant pulsing life of its own.

The seminary studies were tremendously important, wonderfully stimulating—but after all, *this,* the simple "Tending of the Garden," was the whole aim. I suppose, too, I had one very selfish reason for especially enjoying this summer. Until now, Jim's work had been a thing apart, but now he made it plain that he wanted me to share in what he was doing, indeed counted on me for certain things, and I liked being necessary in this way.

Late in June, we returned to Rockwood, where Jim was given both a written and oral examination by the members of Presbytery to determine his fitness to be licensed as a student minister. This was the next formal step before ordination of a minister. He had to submit two rather lengthy papers—and undergo a gruelling quiz on theology and doctrine. The examiners were all old friends of his, and perhaps because of this were determined not to let him off too easily.

"How did it go?" I asked, when he returned from the ordeal.

"Well," he said grimly, "it was no mere formality, I assure you. I think three-quarters of those questions were asked out of sheer devilment—but I answered them."

Before he was licensed, Jim was to preach. "Jane," he said to me, "what shall I say to them? This will be a gathering of the people I love most, and it's the first time I've really been uneasy."

"Why don't you tell them why you went into the ministry?" I asked. "Have you ever publicly said that? That's the question which must lie in their minds."

The church was full when we came in that evening, with the ushers bringing additional chairs to place along the wall and down the aisles. There were friends and relatives on hand from Chattanooga, Knoxville, Sweetwater, Harriman, and Kingston, as well as Rockwood. I poked Jim with my elbow, and whispered, "Well, it looks like they turned out to *hear* whether any good thing came out of Rockwood!"

When Jim began his sermon, I realized that he was, in a way, completing his sermon about the tomatoes, using the same homely, familiar imagery.

When I tried to decide what to say to you tonight, Jane said that most of you would want to know just why I went into the ministry. Now that I have gone this far, the question seems to me not *why* I went into the ministry, but why I waited so long!

You know, when Jane wanted us to buy a farm, I agreed with her that we should have one, but I never really intended to do any farming myself. Then, after we'd been living there a while, on land that was really my own, I was just too Scotch to let it go to waste. Once I had begun to till the soil, once I had planted with my own hands tiny seedlings, nurtured and tended them, fertilized them and hoed around them, and with my own hands picked the fruit of my labors, I found rising within my heart a deep and intense love of the earth, a joy in the labor, and a satisfaction in its fruit.

For years, I had done church work of one kind or another. In the midst of a host of other activities, I did keep my church work first, but it was only a few years ago that I realized that the deepest and most meaningful experiences of my life had *all* come through the church. As I sought out people here and there, and had tried to cultivate in them a love for God, I found that the fruit of my labor brought a great strengthening and enrichment of my own life. As with my garden, I found I reaped an unexpected harvest: a joy and a satisfaction beyond all description. I began to wish I had made the ministry my life's work—and the wish became a clamoring and insistent thing, until, over all sane and sensible objections, I knew I had to do it, that God was somehow calling me late in life for some particular purpose. . . .

In God's sight I am surely nothing much, only a man whom He created, and whom He has seen fail time and again: over and over God has seen me fall short of the things I ought to have done in His service. But there is one small thing I *can* do. I can, in one small place, preach the Gospel. As Christ died for me, I can tell others that He died for them also. Somehow, by my example, I can try to show His love for others, and how faith in Him fills the heart of a man with joy.

Few men will ever hear the sound of my voice, but perhaps *one* who hears may catch the vision more clearly than I have, and go on to tell others, who in their turn, may bear the message to the ends of the earth.

So I am entering the ministry to serve my Lord, to call men to remembrance of Him and His ways, and God willing, I shall spend the rest of my life doing just that.

Meanwhile, there was much going on in our churches. In Lexington, Jim and some of the congregation had worked all through the spring for a new manse. Finally, to Jim's great surprise, the congregation had voted to go ahead with the building. Leaving the meeting, Jim said, "I'm glad they voted to go ahead with the building, but you know, somehow I expected more opposition. It makes me a little uneasy. Perhaps I've just been wrong, and more people really are in favor of it than I thought." Events were to prove, though, that he wasn't wrong.

A hole was dug for the foundation, concrete was poured for the basement floor, and a mason laid the foundation walls. Then men of the congregation helped to tie in the studs and the framework began to rise. As it took shape, it began to look like a house. The roof beams were covered with roofing—and the first fresh enthusiasm seemed suddenly to be gone. Fewer turned out to help, and the building seemed to drag.

"Jim, what's wrong?" I asked. "Why aren't people turning out to work?"

"I don't know, Jane," he said. "I sensed hesitancy about the manse, but when it was put to a vote, the majority was for it. I know they need it, and when we leave, it will help them get a better man. But there's too much of a tendency to let Dale Renschler do it all. It was natural enough for him to be asked to superintend the job—he has more vision and energy than almost anyone else in the church, and he's willing to give more —both in time and money. But they seem to expect him to do it all. I think I'll make a special appeal on Sunday to see if we can't get more help. The whole burden shouldn't be carried by two or three."

The response to Jim's special appeal was disappointing. In the end it was I who inadvertently stung the congregation into action.

I was disgusted when I looked out on Monday morning and saw only three men working. Jim put on his work clothes and went out to help. I decided that if there weren't enough men to help, I would go, so I put on an old pair of slacks and followed him.

The men were a little shocked to see me, and in pants at that. I had brought my own hammer. "Why, Miz Huff," they asked, "what on earth are you going to do?"

"I came to nail up plasterboard. Isn't that what you're doing?"

"Well, yes, ma'am, but. . . ."

They didn't quite dare say more, but it was plain from their faces what they were thinking. I knew they were afraid to let me start. "I can't cut the boards, but I can nail them up," I said. "Here, let me take this one," and I held it up in place, and started nailing along the studs as I had seen them do.

Through the first two pieces they just stood and watched me, but when I had finished the second without denting the board or missing a nail, the men went quietly back to their own jobs, shaking their heads. I worked until mid-morning, when I stopped to fix coffee for them, then went back to work for the rest of the day. The second day more men came out, and by the third my help wasn't really needed any more.

Even so, there was a very obvious failing on the part of the congregation at large to do their part on the manse. What others left undone, Dale Renschler quietly and unassumingly did. He carried the largest part of the financial load as well.

"Jane," Jim said, "Dale has really had to take more than his share on this thing. It's disappointing to watch, and I just hope he doesn't become embittered. If the congregation didn't intend to build the manse, they should have voted against it, rather than voting for it, giving Dale the job of supervising it, and then letting him down."

There was nothing we could say to Dale. He made no comment about it, and invited none. We thought we knew how he felt. But neither of us realized just how deeply Dale had been hurt until he wrote to Jim four years later:

I have never told anyone this before, but when you left Lexington, I had serious thoughts of leaving the church. It was your apparent calm and support that buoyed me up. . . .

If you will remember, the congregation had let us down while building the manse. I thought we would finish the manse and then I would drop out, as I didn't think the people were as sincere in their religion as outwardly appeared. Then I thought, the church is bigger than any one congregation—and I remembered how one man had lost the respect of many people when he had left the church because he had been hurt in a similar way. I decided I couldn't let it be personal, so I would stay.

Also, on a battlefield in Europe I had dedicated my life to God. No one under battle and facing death at any moment is without fear and prayer—the sad part of it was when we would get relieved and go to the rear for a short period. Then most of the boys would forget their promises and would get a bottle of cognac and a girl and have a ball. For myself, being married and much older (and I hope wiser) than most of the boys, I realized a promise to God was not to be taken so lightly. It wasn't a short-term promise for me, either, so I was still under obligation.

It had taken real strength of character for Dale to keep right on working with no word of complaint for what others were not doing.

It is the minister who feels most of the burden of failures in such an instance. He has allowed a project to be initiated when the people are not mature enough to handle it, and must feel the self-reproach of poor judgment. Then I suppose he also faces the temptation to preach about it! Jim didn't, directly, yet I suppose it was underneath much of his thinking as he prepared his sermons.

The summer was all too soon over, the school year beginning again. We decided I would remain at Lexington, to be of more use to our people. The new manse was nearly complete, and we hoped to move into it in October.

Country life has an inescapable lure for me. The eternal quality of the country gives me deep inside the feeling that we have conquered time, captured its essence, and distilled its sweetness.

While the front of our manse faced on the town square of Lexington, the back faced open farm land, and I was happy there. At the farm in Rockwood, I had felt comfortably isolated in the country, but here, I was more or less "on call" during Jim's absences, and because of the summer's visiting, I felt close to my neighbors.

They might at first glance have seemed different from my urban neighbors in Louisville—but as I grew to know them, I saw they knew how to live. They worked very hard to wrest a living from their unyielding land, but they took time to know their neighbors, they seemed to have a sixth sense when help was needed, and came without being called. They held things and time in better perspective than most of my city neighbors. I think it is this quality of perspective that gives so many of us a yearning to live in the country, with its less demanding pace.

Life and death assume a stark reality in rural living, for nothing is hidden there. In the busy city, the tides of humanity ebb and flow so swiftly that a man may die with none to mark his passing. Even his friends may long be unaware of it, for death does not touch us so often when we live in the city.

But in the country, we are all aware of the inexorable march of death, which comes to each of us in time. Only a strong sure faith in Almighty God is proof against the despair it would otherwise leave.

School had been in session for some weeks when Miriam Hensler called to tell me that little Billy Green had been killed that afternoon. Billy and his older brother Claire had caught the school bus home as usual, and the driver had let them out in front of their grandparents' farm. Usually, the driver waited for Claire and Billy to cross the road before going on. This time for some reason Billy did not cross with his brother—but the driver assumed he had, and when he saw Claire was safely out of his way, he started the bus.

He had not taken his hand off the gear shift when he felt a sickening thud, and knew without thought that he had hit little

Billy. In a stultifying agony of horror, he wanted to back the bus away from the child, but the slavery of habit betrayed him. Before he could think of the next movement, his hand completed the shift of gears already begun, and the bus lurched forward over Billy's inert body.

Up on the hill, Billy's grandmother, Mrs. West, had come out when she heard the school bus, and stood helplessly watching the bus hit him, lurch, and then roll over him.

"If you can come now," said Miriam, after she told me these bare details over the phone, "I think it would be a comfort. I'll be glad to come for you."

"Please do. I'll phone Jim. I think he'll want to come up from Louisville."

Miriam was calm when she picked me up but was visibly touched by the tragedy which had befallen her neighbors. I suppose, too, that it came very close to home, for her three children rode the school bus, too. "It is a terrible thing," she said. "The poor driver is ready to die with remorse—he was just too old to be driving the school bus, but no one else wanted the job. Now several hotheads who wouldn't take the job are talking wildly against him, while Mr. and Mrs. West are grieving for little Billy. Billy's mother will come down from Scottsburg as soon as they get in touch with her. It's all such a pity."

She drove skillfully as she talked, down the black-topped road between Lexington and Sharon Hill, turning left over the creek when we sighted the West's house, high on the hill overlooking the road.

Some of the neighbors had tried to get Mrs. West to lie down, but she was so upset she couldn't be quiet. She was still wearing the apron she had on when she stepped out on the porch more than an hour before. She clutched the apron with weary, nervous hands, twisting and turning it unconsciously as she paced the floor, telling again and again the pitiful story of what she had witnessed, as if the telling could wash away the event.

"I've always tried to take care of Billy," she said earnestly.

"I've always tried to do for him what I could. When I looked down and saw what was happening, I wanted to run, but there was no time. I couldn't reach him. I couldn't stop that bus. We've tried to be a family to that boy because he didn't have any father to take care of him and his mother worked. We've tried—and yet I stood there and watched. I screamed, but he couldn't hear me way down there, and anyway, it was too late. I watched him get killed, and I couldn't do a thing."

The apron was twisted into a rope under her hands. Now she untwisted it again, looking with unseeing eyes at the women around her. "She's been talking like this ever since I came," whispered one of them to me.

She was evidently in a state of shock. Her skin was pale and dry, and her eyes stared vacantly. I stepped up to her, wondering how I could get her to lie down before she collapsed. As I came into view, her eyes focused on me. "Why?" she asked. "Why? Why did this have to happen to Billy, and him so little?"

I knew just how she felt. In addition to the loss of a child she loved as if he were her very own, there was a terrible sense of failure in her responsibilities to the child's mother. Yet there was nothing she could have done—and the shock of helplessly watching was almost too much to bear.

How could I help her? *"Lord, give me the words,"* I prayed silently. *"Give me the sense to say something that will comfort her."*

She was little and old and frail, and swayed a bit as if a wind had begun to blow upon her. It was only natural to put my arms around her, then to talk as soothingly as I knew how.

"Mrs. West, I don't know why it had to happen to Billy," I said, "and I don't know why it had to happen where you could watch it and not be able to help." She moved restlessly, and I led her out of the room toward the bedroom, talking as I went. "We do not know whether this was something God allowed to happen, to be used for some purpose, or whether it was after all, only the human, natural mistakes of a man and a boy, which coming together at that time and that place brought tragedy. But this much you do know: you have loved Billy and taken care of him well. You have loved the Lord and served Him as you could. In spite of your heartache and grief, you know that Billy is with God, for you yourself taught him your faith in God. Now you have to leave Billy in God's hands, and you have to put yourself in God's hands. Asking 'why?' won't help. I only know that in my own life I have found God has always taught me something through sorrow. I could never see *what* it was or *why* it was at the time, but when enough time had passed, I could look back and see some gleam of meaning in the experience. . . ."

Mrs. West grew quiet as I talked. Now she seated herself on the edge of the bed. "Why don't you stretch out for a few minutes?" I asked. Wearily, she did, and I pulled up a quilt to cover her.

She had rested only briefly when there was a light knock at the open door—I looked up to see Jim standing there. Why, it had already been more than an hour since I had called him! His warm, compassionate gaze held my eyes for a moment, then he came in to sit in the chair I had pulled up beside Mrs. West, and I left him with her.

Chapter 10

THE FOLLOWING JUNE, at the end of his second year in seminary, Jim was ordained a minister of the Presbyterian Church. Hugh Simon conducted the ordination ceremony, similar to a marriage both in its gravity and in its exaltation. Many ministers attended this most solemn initiation into the service of God.

The formal ceremony began with a catechism of the applicant by the presiding minister. Armed with the authority of the Church, Hugh put each question as a ringing challenge, and Jim steadfastly and unwaveringly made each required response:

"Do you believe in one God, Father, Son and Holy Spirit," Hugh asked, "and do you confess anew the Lord Jesus Christ as your Saviour and Lord, and acknowledge Him Head over all things to the Church, which is His body?"

Jim answered solemnly: "I do so believe."

"Do you believe the Scriptures of the Old and New Testaments to be the Word of God, the only infallible rule of faith and practice?"

"I do so believe."

Question and answer, they went earnestly through the articles of faith, Jim's conviction of his call to the ministry, and desire to promote the glory of God through the gospel of Christ.

Then Hugh signed for Jim to kneel, and every minister in the room came forward silently to stand close by him. Hugh began to pray, praising God for His wisdom in time past, and for the way in which He had ordered and ordained the Church. "Send down thy Holy Spirit upon this Thy servant," he continued, "whom we, in Thy name and in obedience to Thy holy will, do now by the laying on of our hands. . . ." He now placed his hand upon Jim's head, and each of the other ministers also laid a hand upon him. "Ordain and appoint to the office of the holy ministry in Thy Church, committing unto him authority to preach the Word, administer the sacraments, and to bear rule in Thy Church."

It had been busy but a quiet year, of solid accomplishment and deep contentment. So stimulated was Jim by his studies, and so important did he consider them, that he decided to continue and complete the regular three-year course, even though he was ordained.

Our happiness was marred only by the death, after a lingering and painful illness, of Jim's mother. She had a stroke near Christmas, and Jim went home. She then rallied, finally to die in May. Her death was a relief and a blessing, for her last months were filled with pain.

Meanwhile Jim completed, insofar as he was able, the work for which he had come to Lexington. It was his goal that Lexington should have its own, full-time minister. The completion of a new and practical manse was the first step; the next was the separation of the work of the Lexington and Sharon Hill churches. At the end of summer, Jim resigned as student pastor of the Lexington church, in the hope that the people of the church would now support a student minister by themselves, then later secure a full-time minister. In time, this hope became a reality.

Before returning to Louisville in the fall we had a two-week Bible school for the Lexington children and, after we moved, a similar session in Sharon Hill. It was hard work, and meant commuting forty miles to the church each day. The children thrived on it, but Jim looked tired. I was glad he was to work in only one church during his last year at seminary.

As we prepared to begin the new school year, Jim admitted that he was quite tired and needed a rest.

"Well, when are you going to take it?" I challenged him, "this summer is gone."

"Let's take all of next summer and do something lazy with the children—maybe go to a beach somewhere, and just golf and swim and sit and soak up sunshine. Do you know, I've only played golf four times in the last two years?"

"I know," I said. "That's why you've had to take so much more insulin."

In early fall we received a letter from the Children's Agency. In May we had completed Marie's adoption, and I had written to them saying that I knew it was not their policy to place a third child in a home, but that Jim and I still longed for another child. Now they made a most exciting proposal:

Some time ago you wrote us expressing your desire for another child. Since that time, we have given considerable thought to Anne, a little girl just eight months younger than Marie. . . .

As we began to make plans for her adoptive home placement, our pediatrician requested a delay, as he felt a heart condition may exist. . . . She has a short life expectancy but may well live a normal lifetime. . . .

We are asking you to consider giving Anne a free home, without neccessarily adopting her. There is the obvious heartbreak which may be involved for your whole family. . . .

We believe Anne can enrich your life, and certainly she has need of a home and family life such as yours. It will be hard to disassociate pity when making this decision but you must try to do so.

If you are interested in Anne, let us share with you more details about her background and personality. . . .

The thought of another child lifted my heart. "Oh, Jim," I said. "Of course we want her, don't we? And if we take her, we'll have to adopt her. We couldn't get all wrapped up in her, and then know that if anything happened, she could be taken away from us."

"I agree," Jim said. "We'll take the risks as they come. It will be nice for Marie to have a playmate."

I think the case workers at the Children's Agency were a little puzzled by us. We asked the normal questions about Anne's looks and disposition, and Jim did ask if we could be sure Marie wouldn't completely obscure her, for it was very evident that Marie was a gifted child, which could be unfair competition for a child just eight months younger.

"Oh, I don't think you need to worry about that," we were told. "Anne is a very intelligent child. She can hold her own with Marie."

We then asked when we could have her.

"But you haven't asked anything about her heart condition," they objected.

"I thought you had told us all you could in the letter," said Jim. "It really won't make any difference in our wanting her. You see, we feel as you did that she can enrich our life. Beyond that, I can't see that it matters. It isn't pity—we simply want another child, and you say this one could enjoy our home."

Still, we hadn't quite satisfied them. "Have you really considered," they asked, "the effect that her short life expectancy might have on the other children?"

"Why, yes," said Jim. "But death is a fact of life. The children must meet it sooner or later. The way they take it and are affected by it will depend largely on how Jane and I take it.

"We couldn't bear to miss the experience of having another child," he went on, "just because she might be with us only a short while. We would much rather have her for a short while, and love her for that time, than never have her at all."

Apparently they were satisfied. We made a date to see her two days later.

It was one of those days when everything goes wrong. Anne, now twenty months old, had remained far longer than was usual in a temporary foster home because of the uncertainty over her heart condition. Her foster mother had grown to love her dearly. Inevitably, there was heartache involved for the woman who had cared for her, and when the young case worker went to get Anne the woman became hysterical at the prospect of parting with her. Anne, seeing her best friend in tears, also became hysterical. To make things worse, the case worker decided that Anne's long straggling hair made her look pitiful, so she made the mistake of stopping at a barber shop. Anne, already frightened, screamed and fought the barber, her tears and terror multiplied. She emerged with her straight blonde hair in a terribly ragged, short Dutch-boy haircut, half of her little ears showing.

By the time we arrived at the Children's Agency, the distraught case worker had gotten her into clean clothes, but her chubby face, though freshly washed, was still swollen from crying. Both of them looked utterly exhausted. "I'm so sorry," explained the case worker as she led us into the nursery where Anne lay in a crib clutching a bottle. "She is so upset, I don't know what to do. I've never had anything like this happen before."

My heart went out to the little thing. She looked so forlorn lying there. Her hair was so pitiful—but it would grow. Her fat little hands clenched the bottle as if it were the only comfort in her small world. I longed with all my heart to pick her up, but didn't dare, for fear I might frighten her more. But Jim was never a stranger to any child. Speaking softly, he put out his arms to her. In a moment, he had her in his arms, and they were cooing at each other like a pair of lovebirds.

"My," said the case worker, more than a little awed, "I didn't think anyone could do that. I've been wondering how I could ever get her into the car and back to the foster home. Would you . . . would you like to take her on home with you now?"

It was my turn to be startled. I had been so sure they wouldn't let us take her home that day that I had made no preparations.

But Jim answered smoothly, "Why, of course, we'll be glad to."

The young woman was relieved. I don't believe she had intended to send Anne home with us. I think she had just been afraid to upset her more and had spoken because the child was so obviously happy with Jim.

Unfortunately, that was the only place she was happy. If he set her down she screamed, a terrible, frightened, rending scream. He had intended to drive, but she grew so terrified he had to pick her up again. "You drive us home, honey," he said to me. "I'll see if I can't keep her quiet until we get home. She'll be all right as soon as she gets used to us."

It took far longer for her to get used to us than we had dreamed it could. Jim was preparing for tests, and couldn't give her much time. Nothing I could do seemed to interest her at all. She screamed loudly and at length every waking minute, except when she was clutching her bottle.

"Jane," said Jim as he left, "I feel like a heel, leaving you, but I can't hold her forever—not if I'm going to stay in seminary."

"Of course not," I said. "I'll manage."

But this was the most emotionally exhausting experience I had ever been through. The child was so obviously and so terribly upset, and I wanted so badly to take away her fears, to set her at ease, yet there seemed to be nothing I could do for her.

Marie and John were at first fascinated by her performance, then jealous. Marie, who had discarded diapers and bottles a year before, saw Carol Anne getting so much attention that she demanded the same. So I proceeded to put diapers on Marie and to give her a bottle every time I gave Carol one. Marie very quickly grew bored with the routine, and went back to her own more mature ways. But John was not so easily placated. Something about this new child set him wild, and he went into a frenzy of devilment.

Every time I turned around, he was in some new mischief. He refused to go to school, even though he loved to go. He set fires in the house, in the basement, in the alley, watching with glee the coming of the fire department. He found ways to stop up the plumbing and unplug the electrical equipment. I knew these were all bids for attention, and I gave him all the attention I could, trying to make him feel special, hoping that the time would come when he would want to help Carol Anne, rather than hate her.

And still the screaming continued. I had never before realized how penetrating the human voice could be. It tore at my heart until I felt I couldn't bear it another second. There had to be some way to reassure her.

I didn't find the way. It happened just as Jim had said it would. On the eleventh day she woke up, looked around, and apparently decided that if nothing had happened to her yet, it wasn't going to happen. She peacefully ate breakfast with us without making a sound, and when John made a silly face, she laughed at him. Just the simple, spontaneous laughter of a child, but after ten full days of terrified screaming, it was music.

I looked at Jim. "Yes," he nodded, "she's over the hump. You can relax now and begin to enjoy her."

Without realizing it, I had been wound up almost to the breaking point. I had known I was dreadfully tired—but I didn't realize how tired until that moment, when Jim's understanding and reassuring sympathy seemed to loosen a spring. The tears began to roll down my face.

"Hey, I said to relax, not go to pieces." He came over to kiss me goodbye. "Here, honey," and he gave me his handkerchief. "Will you be all right?"

"Yes," I answered, making full use of the handkerchief. "It was just such a relief to hear her laugh. Now if I can assure John he's still Chief Big Feather around here, I'll be more than happy."

Jim broke news so abruptly. "Jane," he announced excitedly only a few days later, "it's a good thing Miss Carol Anne has settled down. Do you think you could manage all the children for a weekend trip?"

"Where?"

"Princeton, Kentucky."

"Where's that, and why?"

"It's a little town about two hundred miles southwest of here, not too far from Paducah. I've promised to preach there on Sunday, and I'd like you and the children to go with me."

"But Jim, why are you going 'way down there?"

He looked a little embarrassed. "Oh, honey, Dr. Hanna has been so insistent that I go down there and preach that I just didn't have the heart to refuse him."

"But you have a church. Why go down there?"

"You ask too many questions. He wants me to go as a candidate. I know you don't like the climate in the Ohio Valley, but that seemed such a poor reason to say I wouldn't go down and at least look at it."

It was late afternoon when we reached the town. The gray stone courthouse threw its shadow toward us as we drove into the square. There was a bustle of cars and people. "This is a shopping center for a fair section of the county," Jim explained, "and most of the farm folks come in on Saturday."

On the southwest side of the square were long, green wooden benches, where old men sat in the bland sunlight, soaking up sun, exchanging yarns and comments on the passing scene. "All the comforts of home, and twice as much to talk about," chuckled Jim. "I'll bet they have to come early in the day to get a place on one of those benches.

"I've got to find the hardware store. The man who runs it is George Eldred and he's treasurer of the church. I'll let him know we're in town, and find out where we're to stay." He spotted the store and maneuvered into a parking place. "You can watch the passing parade, too," he said. "Sorry I couldn't find you a place in the sun."

We settled ourselves in a local motel, and next morning we attended the church service in force.

Outside, I had only a moment to glance at the church, which

was old and built of red brick. Once it must have been imposing and dignified, but long neglect had given it all the charm of an aging factory. Even the joints in the brick needed mortar, and I guessed it was damp and chilly in wet weather. The inside was dreary.

The church was well filled to look over the new preacher, and I was looking them over, too. It was a far nicer-looking congregation than I expected from the appearance of the church. They were well dressed and seemed assured and poised. The service went smoothly under Jim's direction. I could sense warmth and unity, and when Jim spoke, as he always did, with evident love in his heart for his hearers, there was an instant rapport between them.

"God's Man" was his topic. He described Joshua and his calling by God, but he might himself have been the man he described: "Called of God, ready to lead his people, strong and of good courage, steeped in the love and understanding of God's desire for his service."

In the vestibule, George Eldred showed us plans for a big, modern educational plant. It was to be a spacious brick building, with a big fellowship hall and kitchen, Sunday school rooms, even a choir room adjoining the sanctuary. Jim was fascinated.

After lunch we went to see the manse. John D. Reese, who knew the town, had commented when he heard Jim was to preach there, "Well, you'll like the people, but I couldn't ever imagine you and Jane living in that manse. It's really a mess."

He was right. We made only the most perfunctory tour—and that was quite unsettling. The wallpaper had been applied at least thirty years before, the drab, mottled oatmeal variety popular about 1920. The rooms were large but irregular. In several spots the ceiling plaster had parted company with the laths above it and was hanging suspended, awaiting some inconvenient moment to dump itself upon the floor below. Jim asked George Eldred if there would be any objection to a minister's building a house of his own and renting the manse.

When George replied that there would be none, Jim only nodded. He said nothing about his plans, but by the time we left Princeton that day, his mind was made up. If the Princeton congregation wanted him, he would go.

The strain of our first weeks with Carol Anne, together with our long trip to and from Princeton had worn me down more than I realized. I felt vaguely ill for about two weeks after we got back to Louisville. Then I folded up completely.

The doctor was very cheerful. "Pneumonia," he said lightly. "Nowadays it's a lot easier to cure than the common cold. We'll have you up again in a few days."

He was as good as his word. I was up in a few days, all right, but I still felt dreadful. No reason to give in to it, I told myself—and I didn't, for two more weeks.

One morning I got Jim and John off to school, finished feeding the girls their breakfast—and then just couldn't go any further. All of a sudden I felt that my bed was far, far away. It wasn't more than thirty feet from where I stood in the kitchen, but at that moment it seemed like climbing Everest to get across the kitchen, down the hall to my bedroom, and across the room to my bed.

With a tremendous effort of mind and will, I got myself out of the kitchen and down as far as the telephone. I thought foggily, "I'd better phone the doctor while I'm here." I didn't dare sit for fear I couldn't get up again, but leaned against the wall for support while I dialed. The receiver was suddenly too heavy for me to hold in one hand, so I held it painstakingly in both hands.

I was so vague and numb, I was startled when someone answered the phone. Carefully, I gathered my words. "This is Mrs. Huff," I said thickly. "Could you reach the doctor and ask him to come to see me before he comes to the office?"

"Couldn't you come down to the office?" the nurse asked brightly.

There are times when saying the simplest words requires

enormous exertion. "No," I managed finally, "the doctor will have to come here."

"Well, I'll see if I can locate him. But if I don't, you call us again later in the morning."

"That's silly," I thought. "How would I ever walk all those miles to the telephone?" I had no strength left to explain. All I could get out was a weak, "Oh."

"The children," I thought hazily, "I must do something about the children." They had gone into their room and were playing contentedly on the floor. Marie was two and a half, Carol not yet two. I leaned against the wall for a little while, and finally managed to attract Marie's attention. "Marie, Mother has to lie down," I carefully told her. "You and Carol play with your blocks, and when you need anything, come into my room and ask me."

"Yes, Mama," she said happily and ran back to Carol.

Leaning against the wall, I contemplated the awful journey to my bedroom, and when I had thought about it long enough, I set out. I managed it in an upright position, I think, but I have always remembered it as crawling through a long dark tunnel, tilting upward.

For hours I lay drifting at the edge of consciousness. All day I wanted to get up and check on the little girls, but they couldn't even hear me call. They needed food, and their naps, but I was foolishly, completely helpless. "God, how can I get them their lunch?" I asked. "Please help me."

A stranger came to the door. When I didn't answer the bell, she rattled the door, and it came open under her hand.

"Is anyone home?" she called. "Is anyone here?"

Weakly I called, "Come in, come in here."

She was startled when she saw me in bed. She introduced herself and then apologized, "I'm so sorry to bother you. I only came by to get some information."

"You're an answer to prayer," I assured her, and explained my predicament. It only took her a few minutes to phone the doctor's office again, and the seminary to leave word for Jim. She didn't leave until she put the girls into their cribs for a nap. I thought of the good Samaritan, but scarcely got the words out to thank her.

The doctor and Jim came at the same time. "This time," the doctor said, "we'll get you into the hospital, and give you enough penicillin to knock out the pneumonia. I think you got up too early last time."

In three weeks, though, I was no better. "At first, I just thought your case wasn't responding to treatment," said the doctor. "Now, I begin to think you didn't have pneumonia at all."

Tests confirmed the doctor's suspicions. Instead of virus pneumonia, I had infectious hepatitis, a dangerous infection of the liver. I had in fact been ill with it for seven weeks, since our trip to Princeton. Now the blow fell. "You're going to have to stay in bed for six more weeks and be completely inactive," was the doctor's verdict, "and you can't go home until you've made some arrangements for a housekeeper."

We found help for a part of the time—but the turnover of housekeepers proved to be appalling. The apartment *was* quite large, and though the little girls were not much trouble, John set up a special campaign of harassment for each new person who came to work for us. When Jim or I were in sight, John was a model of behavior—but when we were not, he went berserk.

Poor Jim. He couldn't study at home, for he seemed to feel he must be doing something for me or the children every minute he was there. As soon as supper was over, he would settle the little girls in bed, spend a little time with John, then come in to visit with me.

The days and the weeks marched on leaden feet. Christmas came and went. The New Year began. I looked forward to the day when I could get up, but when six weeks ended, I was no better. "Well, let's wait a week or two more," said the doctor—

but at the end of two weeks, there was still no improvement. He called in a specialist for consultation. The specialist discovered that my case was complicated by mononucleosis, a disease of the spleen. I would have to lie flat on my back for at least four weeks, and not even sit up in bed.

I was too disappointed even to cry. I thought I had served my time, and more. I had thought I could get up and begin slowly to take care of Jim, my children, my house—but Jim must still take care of me, and all the rest, too, and it was time for his mid-year exams, besides.

Life grew more complicated than ever. Because, in October, we never dreamed my illness would last so long, Jim had accepted the call from the Princeton church, agreeing to come on the first Sunday in January, and commute between there and Louisville for the remaining five months of the seminary year. He now added the nearly four-hundred-mile round trip to all else he had to do each week.

He took upon himself so many extra tasks for our comfort that it made my heart ache. He was afraid the children were going to be neglected, and watched out for them constantly even when we had help.

My four weeks of lying flat ended—and the laboratory technician came by to take new blood samples. These showed no abatement of the infection. "Just exactly how much longer can this go on?" I asked my doctor.

"Why. . . ." His answer was obviously reluctant. "I have known it to last three or four years."

"Thank you," I said. "It's important to know. I think I'd better start planning for the long haul instead of letting my family go on living from hand to mouth."

What did he mean by three or four years? No one predicted the course of an illness in those terms. Three months ago, he had been rather confident of the outcome. He had been wrong, though he must have spoken in terms usual to recovery. What, then, did this sentence really signify? That I would not get up again? If I were not strong enough to have thrown off the virus in this length of time, what could end it in three years, but death?

Clearly, there could be no other answer. I suddenly recalled a scrap of conversation at a dinner during Jim's first year at seminary. I had stated rather positively what I believed to be the Christian attitude toward death, and had been a little set back when one of the students said bluntly, "You're awfully blasé about it. Maybe you'll sing a different tune when you have to face it."

I now felt almost the same as I had at that dinner table. I believed, "to die is Christ," and that something far better than this earth must await me. I wanted to say, like Paul, ". . . the time of my departure is at hand. I have fought a good fight, I have finished my course, I have kept the faith."

But Paul was sixty when he wrote that passage—at the end of a successful and worthwhile career. I felt I had come only halfway in my career as wife and mother. I wanted to see my children grown. If I died now, what of Carol? We had grown to love her so—but she was not yet legally ours. If I died, they would take her away from Jim. And what of Jim alone, with two children or three to care for? What terrible heartache for him. I could imagine his loss and loneliness. But Jim, at least, would accept. His acceptance would not be simply blind obedience, but the meaningful yielding to the will of a heavenly father. Confident of his strength and courage, I resolved to discuss the future with him.

"Three or four years is an odd way of putting it," I told him. "What do you think he really means? That I'm not going to get up at all?"

"Jane, he said almost the same thing to me," he admitted. "That was what I thought he meant."

"All right, then, let's plan it that way," I said. "First, we can't build a house in Princeton."

"I'd been wondering how to tell you," he said. "What about the manse? It looked pretty wretched to me."

"You'll have to see if the trustees are willing to fix it up.

You know, properly repaired and freshly painted, those big high-ceilinged rooms could be very attractive."

"Do you think so?" he asked eagerly.

I nodded.

"Jane, you write down what you think should be done, and I'll see if they can get it done. If they're willing, we'll plan to move down there just as soon as we can."

I made the list Jim suggested, and he took it to Princeton with him on his next trip. He came back to Louisville glowing. "Jane, they were wonderful. They not only decided to do what you asked, but someone pointed out that we'd have to have an automatic furnace with you sick, and small children in the house. They've already started work!" Truly, the congregation went at the house with a vigor which surprised us both, but which was to prove typical of our people in Princeton.

One afternoon Mrs. Hanna came to call bringing a huge pudding for the children, and for me encouragement. "We've all been very much concerned about you," she said. "I put your name on our special prayer list. There are forty of us women praying for you every day. We hope it's going to be God's Will that you recover and get up again soon. In any case, we're all praying He will strengthen you and help you through whatever comes to you."

What a wonderful warmth she left behind—and how typical of the Christian spirit! Forty women who had never heard of me before this time of need were now lifting my name to Heaven each day, releasing the power of the Spirit of God, that mysterious strengthening spirit which so often works on behalf of those who are receptive to it.

But I had come finally to believe that God's answer to prayers for my recovery was "No." I had faced and accepted the fact that I would be an invalid until I died. Ten days after Mrs. Hanna's visit I was stunned when the doctor came in beaming.

"Well," he said, "you certainly fooled me. After all this time, your tests this week are fine. The whole picture has changed.

You can get up now. You'll have to take it very slowly at first, but the infection seems to be entirely gone. You'll be many months getting back to normal—but you're still mighty lucky."

Free. I was free to come and go as I liked. Free to do for my family, to take care of the children. Free to look after my house. Free to look after Jim. The word rang like an insistent refrain in my head. Free, free, free!

I am afraid I am moderate in theory only. In practice I tend to do most things with all my heart and with all my strength—good or bad. Unfortunately, my strength was no match for my enthusiasm. Four months in bed had left me incredibly weak —and a high carbohydrate diet had left me thirty pounds heavier. My movements were slow, painful, and calculated—I had to plan ahead, work out ways to budget what energy I had.

And there was so very much to do, so many tasks had accumulated in four months. Every closet was a nest of confusion and dirt, the kitchen was filthy, everything was disarranged. But the condition of the house didn't matter half so much as the children. John had a fair amount of freedom and the companionship of other children at school, but it worried me that the little girls were seldom out of the house. Now that I was able to venture forth, I could get them out into the sun—at least for brief periods—and keep them better company.

Through the months I had been in bed, John had gone regularly, alone, down the street to his Cub Scout meetings. I hadn't realized that other parents often attended these meetings, and John minded the fact that I had never come. After school one day he asked if I would take him to one of them.

"But, John, it's only two blocks straight down the street, and you can walk."

"I know, Mom, but I always walk. Most of the other boys come in cars, and their mothers come to get them when it's over."

I could see it was important to John to prove to the other boys that someone cared enough to come after him. I also knew I didn't have strength enough to get myself and the girls to the car twice. "John, why don't you walk down now, and I'll get the girls ready and come after you when the meeting is over. Would that suit you?"

"Yes, Mom," he said eagerly. "But you'll come on in the house, won't you? You won't just wait outside?"

I couldn't help but smile. "All right, son, I'll come into the house—and we'll come a little early."

An hour after he left the phone rang. It was John. "Mrs. Benfield says we're gonna have cake and ice cream today, and she says for you to bring the girls and come down right away." There now. He was not only going to prove he had a mother, but a family as well!

It was a sunny afternoon and the little girls were thrilled at the thought of going to a party. But when we got to the Benfield's house, John had to completely ignore us. He wanted to let it be known he *had* a family, but he couldn't let anyone think he was too dependent on us.

I had met Mrs. Benfield through the seminary. Her husband was minister of the Highland Park Presbyterian Church and also served on the seminary faculty. She had taken a special interest in John. While the children were busy eating ice cream and cake, I had a chance to thank her.

"Oh, John is an interesting child," she said. "We've enjoyed working with him. I'm glad you can get out with him a little. He was so proud you were coming today. How long have you been out of bed?"

"This is my fifth day. I'm still pretty wobbly."

"What a shame you've had such an experience."

"Well, it isn't the kind of experience you'd ever take on voluntarily," I said, "or even wish on your worst enemy, but I guess I've learned enough to make me a better minister's wife. I've always been so stupid about knowing what to do to help people when they were sick. Now, when I go calling I think I'll be able to see what to do."

"What would you do first?"

"I guess I'd do the dishes if they needed doing."

"Oh, I'd never have nerve enough to go into anybody's kitchen," she said.

"Well, once I wouldn't have, but I would now. After lying in bed for months on end, with occasional help and sometimes no help at all, I know how depressing it can be to lie and fret and be helpless to clean your own home. I remember one night when one of my friends came in and found the kitchen a mess. I thought she had left—but found later she had gone in and washed and put away everything in that kitchen. If I hadn't loved her before, I would have loved her for that alone!"

"I see your point. What's the next thing you would do?"

"If there were little children in the house, I think I'd take them out and do something with them. So many times while I was in bed my children couldn't even go out into the back yard, because there was no one to put their snowsuits on or watch them after they got outside. Sympathy is nice, but when you're as sick as I was, what you really need is help," I concluded. "It's a lesson I hope I never forget."

Chapter 11

J IM LOOKED AROUND the crowded station wagon. The children were on the front seat beside him, while I was stretched out full length on a mattress in the rear, surrounded by household gear. "Do we have everything?" he asked. "Then it looks like we're ready. Let's have a short prayer that we have a safe journey and not harm any living creature on our way."

It was March and we were off to Princeton. We had sold the apartment house. Though we would have preferred to postpone the move for a little while, until I was stronger, the new owner needed our apartment, so we moved on schedule.

Moving is always difficult; there is no way to escape the physical and emotional wrench involved. This time was no exception. A magnificent job had been done on restoring the manse, but when we arrived with our caravan of children and possessions, the finishing touches were still being put on it. Our first days were chaos. I was determined that Jim was not going to have to take responsibility for setting up housekeeping —he was to spend his weekdays in Louisville and commute to Princeton only on weekends for the rest of the school year —but my strength was limited, and I knew it would take a while to set my house in order.

The unpacking and settling in, getting the children to feel at home in strange surroundings, and my very definite physical limitations—all together could have been very miserable. But our problems really seemed negligible, for we were almost overwhelmed with kindness.

Princeton should happen to everyone. For all of us there are some places where we are so warmly received that we are immediately at ease. Then, relaxed and comfortable, we can be that person whom we most want to be, and the assurance which comes to us from being loved is so great we can almost literally do no wrong.

Princeton was for me such a place. The gray little town I had seen in the October sunlight proved in March to be rich and colorful in its people and in the experiences it had to offer us.

One day I was lying in bed (where I still had to spend most of the day) reading to John. The house was still full of carpenters and painters, and we had retreated to my bedroom to leave them in peace. Suddenly John looked up and said, "Someone's here, Mother."

Standing in the doorway was an attractive, friendly woman, bearing an apple pie. "I'm Rosalind Young," she said. "I knocked downstairs, and the workmen told me I'd find you up here. I thought the children would enjoy a pie, and I wanted to come to visit a few minutes with you."

"I'll enjoy the pie, too, and the children will be thrilled. I just barely cover the necessary parts of the meals; desserts have grown very rare around here."

Angeline Henry came next, a dear little brown wren of a woman. "I'm Mr. Frank Wood's sister-in-law," she explained, a reference which at first made no impression. ("Who is Mr. Frank Wood?" I asked Jim when he came home. "Oh, honey, Mr. Frank is the reason I'm going to stay in Princeton the rest of my life. Mr. Frank is seventy-nine, looks fifty-nine, sings in the choir, teaches a Sunday school class for me, and dresses like an English gentleman. In short, he's delightful!")

Tiny, trim, bright-eyed Betsy Morgan, the woman who was to become my close friend because of our closeness in interests and even in age (she was four months my junior), came one evening bearing a complete dinner on a tray. "I'm coming later for a real visit," she explained. "This is just to welcome you and give you a rest for one meal," and she breezed away.

Quiet, soft-spoken Anne Sparks brought a great bowl of fresh fruit she had prepared: chunks of fresh pineapple with slices of oranges and grapefruit. "I thought this would be something Mr. Huff would enjoy," she said. "There's no sugar in it." I knew how much time had gone into the peeling and preparing of it, and I was touched by her thoughtfulness.

Most people found me flat in bed; I had to spend a most unseemly amount of time there. The bell rang one day while I was resting, and someone called "Hello" from the front door.

"Who comes?" I asked.

"John D. Reese."

"Oh, come on in," I called. "I'm in bed, and I won't get up for you."

John D. had visited us so often in Louisville that he seemed a member of the family. He was a classmate of Jim's and shared rooms with him at the seminary. While I was ill, he had come out to the apartment to help—from polishing the children's shoes, to bringing a crew of fellows from seminary to pack our books before we moved—so I wasn't at all embarrassed to have him come back to the bedroom. However, I *was* embarrassed to find he was accompanied by two other student ministers, and a plain, graying woman in her fifties, whose face radiated a sweetness and strength of character.

"Well, I'd have gotten up if I'd known you were bringing in a delegation."

"That's why I didn't tell you. Stay where you're comfortable, and you'll get well that much sooner. This is Lillian Abnett, and you already know the boys."

Jim had told me about Mrs. Abnett. She was the only full-time worker for the five parish churches which Jim moderated, and which were served part-time by student ministers. Mrs.

Abnett had been a Christian Education worker for many years, had then met and married a Presbyterian minister some years older than she. After his death, she had offered her services to the board of home missions, asking only that she be sent where there was a special need.

She had been working in the parish for some years, filling the gaps in the work done by the students, mothering them, and serving in the various communities between Princeton and Marion, about thirty miles away. She was a staunch Christian, a woman of integrity, with a nice sense of humor. I was to see much of her in time to come.

The four of them made themselves at home, until Jim came in with the children, then they talked of parish business.

Those first months in Princeton were physically tiring to me: I had so little strength, and was still in a great deal of pain—yet it was a happy time. I had a sense of belonging, of kinship with the people. I loved them, and felt I was loved in return.

I was glad when the school year ended, and Jim came to Princeton for good. He brought home his desk and chairs and books, settled them in the study upstairs under the eaves, and had a telephone extension put in. This telephone was a problem for a while. Carol Anne developed an uncanny instinct for knowing when it was in use, and if I weren't close, she liked to pick it up and chatter into it.

Jim would say, "Carol, put down the phone." But Carol, at two, was much too happy at finding this little black toy would say her name, and she would continue to talk to it. "Carol Anne," Jim would stay patiently, "this is your daddy, put down the telephone." Carol's answer to this was joyous laughter. She *knew* her daddy was much too big to fit in that little black toy, so it was all a joke by the little man who lived inside. No amount of explanation satisfied her. Finally, daddy came down the stairs one day to administer a light spanking—more insult than injury—which persuaded Carol that the "little man" *was* somehow also her daddy.

"Having my study at home is going to be a problem, Jane," Jim said, "but it won't be for long. We have well over half the money for the educational plant in hand now, and I hope the congregation is going to vote a bond issue to raise the rest of it right away. It will only be a matter of months until we have our building, with a regular office."

A few days later Jim wrote jubilantly to his classmate and friend Jim Thorn, now in his own first church. "We got started tearing down the cottage next to the church this morning. That means construction on the new addition can begin on Monday. Did I tell you we sold the bonds we needed right in our own church? I think this pretty good, because those same people are going to have to give the money to pay themselves off! When you stop to think about it, even the interest isn't going to cost us anything!" This was written frivolously, of course, to mask Jim's pride in his people for raising money without going outside the church.

The chairman of the building committee was Carl Sparks, whose wife Anne had been one of the kind visitors during my first days in Princeton. Carl was not a member of the church, although Anne was, and he attended regularly. He became very enthusiastic about this project, however, and gave endlessly of his time to oversee every detail. I wondered at the time how he could be so devoted to the church and yet not want to join it as a full communicant. I was not to discover the reason until later.

The days quickly assumed a pattern. We rose as early as we ever had. We hadn't left the mill whistle behind, for Princeton had its hosiery mill, too, run by an old friend, Grayson Harralson. Jim was usually up before the early whistle blew to go upstairs to his study and work until it was time to go calling. With three sermons a week to prepare, his study could not be done in any haphazard fashion; it had to be a daily discipline.

His first errand after leaving the study was to go downtown to see the progress the builders were making. I didn't realize it at the time, but even these short excursions into town were an active part of his work. The ministry just isn't limited to a forty-hour week, or even a forty-eight-hour week, but is a continuing process, active wherever and whenever the minister is with other human beings. A soldier may take off his uniform and become a private citizen on his hours off—not so a soldier of Christ: he is always "on parade," even in his private life.

Furthermore, it was just impossible for Jim to walk by his townspeople without speaking, and his genuine friendliness and interest inevitably drew a warm response. It wasn't long before Jim knew as much about Princeton as he had known about Rockwood.

The afternoons were almost invariably spent in pastoral calling. If a minister's preaching is his time for making plain his faith to his congregation, then his pastoral calling is the time for listening to his people in return. His calls often continued into the evening, and all too often church and community meetings kept him out late at night.

Jim was proud of the manse, pleased with the congregation for the job they had done in renovating it. They had spent far more than we dreamed would be necessary, but once they had begun the job, they wanted to see it through in the best possible way. We owed much to the personal supervision of Mr. R. A. Willard, whose steady efficiency got everything done quickly and well. In addition to repairing and painting the walls, they had laid new floors in several rooms, refinished the floors through the rest of the house, put in a new furnace and an extra bath, and modernized the kitchen.

"Jane," Jim asked when he moved in permanently in June,

"are you strong enough to manage an open house? I'd like to give everyone a chance to come in and see what has been done. It would be a way of saying 'thank you.' "

"I'd love to," I said. "I can manage by preparing things a little at a time and freezing them. You go ahead and make the invitation."

From the pulpit the following Sunday, he invited the congregation to come and bring their friends. "Mrs. Huff and I are so thrilled with the changes in the manse," he said, "and so touched by your concern for our comfort and welfare, that we want all of you to come and enjoy it with us. We want to thank each of you who had a part in the work, and hope to make this an occasion where we can get to know all of you a little better."

The party was fun. Everything went well, from the weather to the flowers and refreshments, and as host, Jim was at his exuberant, witty best. Because I hadn't met many of the people who came, Jim stayed close by my side to introduce them. Once, though, I missed him for almost half an hour, and his disappearance made me uneasy. I asked George Eldred if he had seen Jim.

"Yes." He began to laugh. "He's upstairs in his study, showing everybody how he studies in that reclining chair. Everybody's taking turns sitting in it."

I had to laugh, too. We had gotten Jim a rather complicated adjustable chair for him to study in comfortably, and it had been a minor wonder in Jim's room at seminary. Now that he had shown it off here, nobody was going to believe he studied as much as he really did. He reappeared a minute later, boyish and exultant, winking at me to acknowledge his dereliction of duty.

I could not help worrying about Jim. The end of his seminary studies should have left him with some time for relaxation and the exercise that was so good for him. But very quickly, it seemed, his time was as completely occupied with pastoral duties in Princeton as it had been in his days of traveling to and from Louisville every week. He looked ever more tired, but he refused to spare himself.

The second Saturday night in June, we drove fifteen miles from Princeton to Bethel, a country Presbyterian church too small to support a minister of its own, or even partially support a student minister. Members of the Princeton church had helped to start the church, and several of the Princeton ministers had helped by holding services there. Because the Princeton church had both morning and evening services on Sunday, another time had to be found for services at Bethel. The congregation had decided on Saturday night.

The church was a simple, sturdy, one-room building. The service began at dusk. The front of the church was lighted by a naked bulb hanging directly over the pulpit. The light was not too noticeable in the last bright flush of sunset, but as the darkness thickened, the light bulb above Jim's head seemed to grow brighter, drawing from the night a thousand assorted bugs which flew in the unscreened windows, dividing their attentions between the light bulb and Jim's head.

How Jim continued the service with unruffled dignity, I do not know. I was aching with the effort not to laugh. Before pronouncing the benediction, he announced that there would be a meeting of the elders immediately.

While the men met, I busied myself getting to know the wives. They were farm people who had come from miles around to fill the little church, and were touchingly pleased that someone was willing to come again to preach to them, for they had been without regular services for many months.

On our way home, I innocently asked Jim what his meeting was about. "What do you think it was about?" he exploded. "I told the men they'd have to get together and make some screens for that church before next Saturday, that I wasn't going to preach another sermon with that army of insects dive-bombing my bald spot!"

The men did build screens, and put them up by the following Saturday, so Jim was able to preach without distraction the rest of the summer.

I loved the simple country services and the kindliness of the people. This church was as plain as a building could be, yet the people came with eager hearts to have the Word preached to them. As we worshiped together, we had the sense of being in a holy place—of sharing a reverence for things unseen and not always understood—things still necessary to the completeness of life's experience.

The pace of Jim's life became more and more demanding. Besides his duties to his own congregation and to the little congregation at Bethel, he worked as moderator of the Parish Council, with five small churches in the parish, supervising the activities of the two student ministers who served them. He took an active part in the Presbytery of which the Princeton church was a member. He was also deeply involved in such community affairs as Kiwanis and the local Red Cross. When I protested about the extras, Jim replied that he had a personal responsibility as a Christian to take his part in community affairs. How else could he influence them?

He was now preaching four different sermons a week, three at Princeton and one at Bethel. Each of these took a great deal of work. Every minister wants to preach good sermons. One good sermon can reach more people than a man can reach in many weeks of personal calling, and any honest, conscientious minister feels it his obligation to give the best of himself in his worship services. It took Jim from ten days to two weeks to prepare one sermon. He always seemed to have several "in process," on little sheaves of note cards, left over from the large store he had bought in seminary. His most intensive work was done in early morning hours in the peace of his study. When he was interrupted, the cards went into a pocket, a rubber band around the cards belonging to each separate sermon, to be pulled out and reread and revised at the first possible moment. He crammed in bits of study through the day, when he could find a minute to begin again. He had the happy faculty of being able to take up where he had left off and going on with his preparation wherever he happened to find himself.

I enjoyed Jim's preaching. I suppose it was because he seemed to love to share from the pulpit his own great love of Christ. There was nothing spectacular about his manner—but he had the gift of making us see the essence of life through the commonplace. I knew that most of his sermons grew out of his own experience, or those of his congregation, and were directed toward questions or perplexities which concerned them.

Everything in life furnished sermon material. One day when several of us were comparing notes on visits to Canada, our friend and neighbor, Elizabeth Woolwine, mentioned the dangerous potholes on the glacier above Lake Louise. Jim and I, on a trip to Canada, had been similarly warned about them, and Jim used them as a forceful illustration a week or two later.

Some of you have asked me why it is that we talk so much in the Church about sin. It is, after all, an unpopular word today. It's likely none of us are murderers, and only rarely do church members steal (though when they are caught at it, it usually makes national headlines). We hope that none of us commits adultery. In short, though there are at times a few backsliders among us, we like to think that by and large our church members are really pretty good people. Why, then, do we talk so much about sin?

It's true that we may not too often have to be concerned about the things which are most often labeled sins. After all, these are the things which *any* sensible citizen, in his right mind, will avoid to keep out of the clutches of the law. The things which we so-called "good" people have to watch out for sometimes seem to be as trivial as a grain of sand. But a grain of sand can sometimes do an extraordinary amount of damage.

When my wife and I were in Canada several years ago, we were told that no one must go up on the glacier above Lake Louise without a guide. They pointed out the apparently flawless surface of the ice and warned us not to trust that glittering expanse. A tiny grain of sand, borne by the wind to the glacier, could at times lodge upon the surface of the ice and melt the ice just beneath it. Then, as it settled to the bottom of the drop of water thus made, it would be caught in a revolving motion which would in turn scour and dissolve more ice. Its motion could continue until a great hole had been carved beneath the ice where the tiny grain had entered, a hole so deep that a man, seeing the apparently perfect surface of the ice, and putting his trust in it, might lose his life in the emptiness beneath.

The sins which are the greatest pitfalls of the Christian life are frequently on the surface as trivial and innocuous as grains of sand on the surface of the glacier. It is what they do to us that makes them important. There are those which lodge lightly on the surface and do no harm, but there are others which sink beneath the surface and are continually in motion, scouring away the heart and soul of a man until there is nothing left within but emptiness.

We cannot make a list of the things which do this to a man, for nothing is, of itself, necessarily wrong, but is to be judged by what it does to us. Whatever scours out of our hearts the love of God is wrong.

Among the "hollow men" of our generation, there are those who have pursued material ends to the exclusion of all else, and now wonder why they can find no meaning in life. All of us are prone to this temptation at times. The world is so much with us, the physical and material needs of our families are so immediate, that we often fall unthinkingly into the pattern of the world around us, going round and round in the circles we know so well, leaving a yawning and aching void under a surface that is apparently whole.

That is why we speak of sin. If we are to grow in love and fellowship with God, and to have the abundant life God intends

for us, we must remove, even from the surface of our lives, anything which can enter in and separate us from the love of God.
Sin is just that: *anything* which can separate us from the love of God.

It was Betsy Morgan who told us the story of two elderly
ladies who decided to take a trip in their equally elderly car
from their home in Kentucky to south Florida. Everyone who
knew them was quite nervous about their making the long trip
safely, but the little old ladies went and returned in good order.
"Did you have any trouble on the trip?" someone asked.
"Not a bit," beamed the voyagers. "We just got on that white
line in the middle of the road and stayed there all the way."
Jim pirated the story, with apologies to Betsy.

I've met those old ladies, and I'm sure you have, too, and have
taken to the shoulder of the road to avoid them, muttering all
the while about the kind of people who were allowed to drive,
as they went their way unheeding. It's easy enough to see another's
mistake and complain about it.
Unfortunately, though, all of us are at times like the two old
ladies. Sometimes when we should choose one side or the other,
we stick to the white line in the middle of the road, and oblivious
of the danger to ourselves and others, ride on unheeding. We try to
straddle a middle ground between the world and the Kingdom of
God—we find it the path that leads to destruction.

After the service I would follow the rest of the congregation
to the vestibule, where Jim would be greeting and shaking
hands with every person. We always gravely shook hands as
I passed. "Mrs. Huff," he would say formally, "we did enjoy
having you worship with us this morning." But his eyes would
be asking questions: *"Was it right?"* or *"Forgive me for telling
that story on you, but wasn't it a good illustration?"*

For months our John had been having troubles—not just
those of adjusting to Carol's arrival in our family, but deeper
ones as well. He had always been a wind that blew from every

quarter—boisterous, energetic, but lacking any scrap of the ability to concentrate or to focus his attention on anything. We knew he was bright, but so acute had his academic problems become that we had finally decided to have him privately tutored. Since coming to Princeton, I had done much of this job myself.

We were sure some of John's difficulties lay in his vision. Not long before we moved to Princeton we learned definitely he was suffering from split vision. No wonder the poor boy hated to read and seemed incapable of studying! At the time, though, he was so upset over my illness that the necessary surgery was out of the question.

Finally, in May, John seemed calm enough to face an operation, so, at Jim's suggestion, I took him to Nashville to see Dr. Henry Carroll Smith. Dr. Smith had, as a child, lived next door to the Huffs in Rockwood. He was an ophthalmologist, who taught in Vanderbilt's medical school, and headed the work in Vanderbilt Hospital's wonderful eye clinic. He confirmed our belief that John needed surgery.

Late June proved to be the best time for us. I didn't tell John until the day before the operation, as I knew he would dread it. Both of us had all-too-vivid memories of his violent reaction to anesthesia when his tonsils were removed. He fought it violently, sinking at last into unconsciousness with groans and sobs. He returned to consciousness screaming, fighting, and dreadfully nauseated. When it was time to tell him, I explained carefully that one reason he was unhappy was because he couldn't see the way other people did, to tie his shoelaces easily or to catch a ball. "We have found a way to fix your eyes so they will work the way they should," I said, "but we have to take you to the hospital to do it. You will be there nine days, and when we bring you home, you will find that things are different, and look different. It won't be easy, but it will be so wonderful to see afterwards."

"Will I have to breathe that nasty stuff again?"

"Do you mean ether? Yes, I'm afraid so. That is the only way they can put you to sleep so you will be quiet during the operation."

When Carroll came out of surgery he told us he found more trouble than he had anticipated. "It's amazing," he said, "that the child's eyes were normal in appearance. No one will ever know just how much he has had to fight against."

Poor John. His recovery from the anesthetic was more violent and terrible than it had been the last time. Added to that was the shock of being completely blindfolded by bandages. No telling could really prepare him for the experience of not being able to see at all. Finally, his sunny disposition asserted itself, and he was all right.

Eight days after surgery, his bandages and stitches were removed, and we took him home. John said it didn't seem too different at first, but almost the first thing he did when he got home was to put together a small model airplane. It was the first time he had either been able to sit still long enough or see well enough to perform such a feat. Jim and I were thrilled, though we knew he might still have to have a second or even a third operation before the correction in his vision was complete.

It was the third consecutive year that Kentucky was parched with drought. The unremitting sun shone day after day until the earth baked and cracked open. With every vagrant breeze, a haze of dust rose from the earth. Old trees with roots halfway to China died from lack of moisture. New shrubs were seared in the hot sun, and all the crops were ruined.

All during the long hot summer, Jim continued on his rounds, preaching and teaching, visiting and working with people in every way he knew. He was happy, but I looked forward to our vacation in August, when he would have time for

more exercise, swimming and golfing,—time enough to let
go for a while.

Many of our church members were farmers, or owned farms,
and many of the businesses in town were dependent to a large
measure on farm trade. The farmers in our congregation were
worried and distressed by the drought; businessmen were tired
from the heat and blue over the lack of trade.

Jim walked all over town and rode through the countryside,
talking to people, talking, talking. As was his way, he left them
refreshed, more hopeful, but he himself looked more tired.
The heat seemed to sap his energy and drain him. More than
ever I was sorry he had not taken the promised three months'
vacation before starting to work. At least, we would have
August. But when I mentioned it to him, he said, "Oh, Jane,
we can't take a vacation this year. So many folks in our congregation are having a bad time just now. Besides, I haven't
been here long enough to warrant taking a vacation."

"But you *need* a rest so badly."

"I simply cannot do it. People need a minister badly in times
like these. I've got to stay."

I could see why Jim wanted to stay in Princeton, but I also
knew he was extraordinarily tired. He no longer seemed to
have the resilience he used to.

A few weeks later the Kiwanis and Rotary clubs staged a
charity softball game. Jim mentioned so off-handedly that he
could pitch, that the manager decided not to take a chance on
the preacher until the ninth inning, when the game was already
lost. Jim managed to put three men out in short order, and
when he came up to bat, swatted one nice hit. Everyone was
most impressed. But when we reached the car afterward, Jim
handed me the keys, saying, "Whew, you'll have to drive. I
didn't think I was going to get clear to first when I ran, and
I really wasn't sorry the next man struck out. I don't think
I could've sprinted to second. I must be getting old. My legs
have really given out." I looked at him sharply, and he turned

away from me, but in the gathering dusk I could see his face was gray.

When summer ended, a short spell of rain brought the promise of another crop in another season. The fields were tilled again, and winter wheat and legumes were planted.

John seemed much more settled since his operation, so we let him enter public school. With the coming of cooler weather, Jim seemed to feel much better. Some of his old vitality returned. Certainly he was happy in what he was doing. He seemed to radiate a deep inner peace, as if he found here in his work with people a fulfillment of all of life's purposes.

In the four short months since Jim had completed his studies at seminary, much had been accomplished. The little Sunday-school house had been torn down, and work was progressing well on the new educational building. The men were getting organized into a program of work and study which seemed likely to awaken in them a new sense of the possibilities and challenge of personal service. With Jim's help we had started a Junior Christian Endeavor group for the children. Jim now had the "feel" of his church. He was a part of the community and had wider involvement out into the county through the parish churches.

For me, the future augured well. My strength was still extremely limited, but I had learned to use it where it counted. I had now been up for six months without any new trouble, and was confident I would continue to grow stronger until I was back to normal.

The little girls were growing so delightfully—we couldn't quite remember what life had been like without them.

As I recalled how happy we had been in our last year in Rockwood, it amazed me to realize how much happier we were now. I realized that just as Jim through the years had believed in me, and seen talents and abilities which I never dreamed I had, so does God believe in us whom He has created. He knows we can do more than we have ever tried, that we can live at a level far beyond what we have yet achieved, and He stirs our hearts to a restless yearning which is never fully satisfied.

What did the future hold for us? Only God knew. But He had led us here, and here we were happy. We had each other, three children we loved, and our greater "family" in the Princeton church, the parish churches, and Bethel. There stretched before us years of work and growth. Truly, our cup ran over, and God had shown us His goodness and mercy in special ways.

BOOK III

THE CRUCIBLE

"The crucible is for silver,
and the furnace is for gold,
and the Lord tries hearts."

PROVERBS 17:3

Chapter 12

In OCTOBER we had a few beautiful fall days. Jim rounded up all the Junior Endeavor members for a hike on the Dawson Bluffs. I was still not up to hiking, so one of our friends took my station wagon loaded with youngsters, and Jim took the rest in his.

They parked near the Bluffs, then hiked up. On the way, they found some grapevines, and cut one end loose to make a marvelous grapevine swing. The children spent half an hour grabbing the end of the grapevine and swinging across a dry creek bed. A bow and some arrows had been brought along and each child was given a chance to shoot.

At the top of the Bluffs, they all stopped for a snack, then after Jim had taken pictures of the group, they hiked back to the station wagons again.

The little girls were in the tub, and I was on my knees beside it when I heard the front door open, and John came whooping down the hall. "We're home, Mom!" he shouted.

"Fine, son. Where's your daddy?"

"He went in your room."

When I had the girls out of the tub, and dried and powdered and clothed, I went to find Jim. He was stretched out on the bed, his face drawn and weary. "Why, Jim, what's wrong? What has happened to you?"

"Just tired, baby. I seem to have overdone it today. My legs don't want to hold me up."

He was quiet while I massaged him. Then he seemed to feel better, and I thought no more of it.

In November it turned raw and cold, and Jim caught a dreadful cold. I thought he should see a doctor, but in the pressure of work he put it off, and the cold persisted until Christmas. I had hoped Jim might rest after Christmas, but we went to visit his family in Rockwood instead.

Jim's cold grew steadily worse, so we said our goodbyes early and started home. Jim began driving, but suddenly felt ill. Quietly, so as not to disturb the children, we checked over his symptoms, for a diabetic's illnesses can be caused by any of a number of routine problems. We decided that he might be having an insulin reaction.

We stopped to eat, thinking that would put an end to the reaction, but Jim was scarcely able to get through the meal. He found it difficult to wait for the children to finish, and finally went out. The close air of the restaurant was too much for him. I rushed the uncomprehending children through their meal and followed him.

I found Jim in the street, between the diagonally parked cars. He had gotten as far as the door of the station wagon, and there he stood in the dreary cold, leaning weakly against the car as if he would topple over without support. I was so startled that I stopped and just looked at him, *really* looked at him—not with the usual glance of loving familiarity, but a sudden, honest searching of his face that shocked me in what it revealed. Jim had aged ten years in the last few months. Gone was the youthful, roseate, boyish look I had always associated with him. The flesh had dropped away from his face, and the skin lay loosely over his bones. He looked white and weary. This was no insulin reaction. Jim was ill.

I was herding the children into the car while he stood there. Above all I didn't want to alarm the children. "Jim, you look bad," I said urgently. "We ought not to go until you feel better.

Let's check with Uncle George, and see if he can't do something for you."

"No, Jane," he replied. "I just asked for three days off, and I want to get back to Princeton tonight. I'll be all right as soon as we get going. . . . But, baby, do you think you can drive?"

Jim had babied me so on the trip to Rockwood, making me stretch out full length on a mattress in the back of the car, that it was shocking now to hear him ask me to do the driving. I was more alarmed than I cared to admit.

I took the wheel, and he sat on the right side, but we had scarcely gotten out of town before I was sure he was too sick to go on.

"Jim, I'm going back to Rockwood. You need help."

"No, baby, go on to Chattanooga. I haven't been feeling well for a long time. Seems like I've had this cough forever. I might as well go on down and let White give me a thorough check up."

We were still sixty-five miles from Jim's doctor brother-in-law in Chattanooga, only five from Rockwood. I hesitated, but Jim was firm. Finally, foolishly, I gave in.

"If you'll lie down, I'll go on." His acquiescence, however, only added to my alarm. He took my bed in the back, and we rode on. I drove as fast as I dared. Fortunately I made good time.

When I got Jim to White's office, he was completely exhausted. White took one look at him and called the hospital for a room.

The efficiency of modern medicine is a wonder to behold. I drove Jim to the hospital, pulled up to the emergency entrance, and Jim was helped into a wheel chair by waiting nurses.

We had phoned Jim's sister Claire from White's office, and she took the three children so I could stay with Jim. We knew we were in for a siege, so she drove the little girls right back to Rockwood, while John was to stay with her and the boys.

Meanwhile, in the hospital, Jim was subjected to a number of tests. He had evidently been walking around with pneumonia for some weeks, and the resulting strain had played havoc with his system. The tests also showed he was seriously anemic and had apparently been so for at least a year—which accounted for his being so tired and so easily winded.

"Just how bad is it?" I asked White.

"It will depend on how badly his kidneys are affected."

"Oh." This was it. Before I heard the rest, I knew this was the beginning of the end. It was no mere presentiment, but a certain conviction. Jim had been ill many times before, but then I had always felt that his tremendous vitality and resilience would restore him to health. It was not that way now. The vitality and resilience were gone. The years of diabetes, the great physical demands constantly made upon him, had taken their toll. My heart cried out inside me, *"Oh, Jim, you said we'd have twenty-five years together—and we've had only nine...."* Man proposes, God disposes. I'd have to take what I could.

There wasn't time to dwell on these thoughts, for White was still talking: "Jim has a seriously strained heart. He is never to lift anything heavy again...." The little girls were going to find it hard to understand why Daddy couldn't swing them from his shoulders any more. John was going to miss all the wonderful rough and tumble wrestling with his father.

And I? Nine years hadn't been long enough—not half long enough. My heart ached with the knowledge that there was only a little more time left. I prayed inwardly for strength to face the ordeal to come.

I went back to the hospital, and massaged Jim until he was relaxed and comfortable. When he drifted off into a natural sleep, I sat beside him, watching as he slept, while whole blood, wonderful, life-giving blood, was slowly put into his veins to restore him to strength again.

In addition to the pneumonia and strained heart, Jim had a severe and complicated form of nephritis. Because he had not had a physical check up in over a year, the nephritis had been unchecked for too long and had done serious damage to the kidneys. It was this which had caused the anemia, and was later to produce even more painful acute swelling of the body.

Medication, and above all, whole blood, alleviated the symptoms temporarily—but nothing could restore the damaged kidneys.

Day after day transfusions were given to him, slowly, drop by drop, carefully administered so they would not overstrain his tired heart. On some days, he could take a full pint, or even a pint and a half. On other days, half a pint seemed too much for his body to absorb.

A friend, Sherwood Dudley, went down unasked to the Blood Bank and left a pint of blood in Jim's name. I thought it was such a nice thing for him to do—I was to appreciate the voluntary gift more and more in the days to come. New blood was needed each week, and it became ever more difficult to obtain. Blood is something you can't just buy; someone must first give it!

As the days went by, Jim began to regain his color and a bit of his strength. Then in Rockwood, Marie came down with the mumps! I had to go to Rockwood to care for her, so I went back to the little girls, sending John by bus to the care of friends in Princeton, so he could get back into school. Claire promised to do the hospital visiting with Jim. How many helping hands it takes to get through illness!

Jim was at last able to leave the hospital, and Claire took him to stay with her until we should all be able to go home to Princeton. When Marie was well enough to travel, Claire brought Jim up so we could leave from Rockwood. It was bitterly cold, and when Jim got out of the car wearing no socks or shoes, only slippers, I was shocked. But I was even more shocked as I realized why he wasn't wearing shoes and socks: his feet and ankles were so swollen he couldn't have gotten them on! *"Oh, Jim! Oh, Jim! It's going to be long and slow, isn't it? A little here, a little there, until like the threads that bound Gulliver, all the little things mount up to make you immobile. Oh, love, I'm so sorry."*

Jim saw my distress about his feet, wrinkled his nose in a gesture that was half deprecation, half sympathy. "You'd better go down to the mill and see if they have any socks large enough to cover them, honey," he said lightly. "And while you're out, please pick up some new road maps. There must be a shorter route back to Princeton."

Louise loaned me more blankets to cover Jim—for he couldn't sit up for the five-hour journey home. Though he protested vehemently, he had to stretch out again on my mattress.

I pretended to have no sympathy at all: "Shut up, man. Now you know how ignominious I've felt all these months when you've waited on me hand and foot!"

"Does that mean you're strong now? It's more a case of the blind leading the blind!"

I was so glad we were all ready to go home, I thought I could do it. I was wrong! Actually, none of the four of us was fit to drive, but I came closest to qualifying. I was anxious to get back to John, to get the girls settled at home again, and just having us all at home would make life *seem* normal, whether it was or not.

Despite the new route, the trip was arduous. By the time we reached home, I was exhausted and feeling ill myself.

When I got into the house, I phoned a friend to come unload the car as I could not, and called the doctor. Then I fell into bed.

Ralph Cash, our doctor, came at once. "You just have a touch of flu. Stay in bed for three or four days."

"But I can't stay in bed."

"Well," he said dryly, "you aren't going to get very far out of it."

And I didn't. We found help, and I got up only when I had to.

Despite my entreaties Jim got himself going again through sheer will power. He was up often in the night, racked with coughing, but when day came he was up as usual and off to the church at his regular hour, making his rounds of the congregation and visiting others outside the church who had some special need. Though it literally took weeks from the pitifully small store of his life, nothing could keep him from his duty.

I could not imagine a life without Jim Huff. Oh, when I was old, perhaps, but when I was thirty-two? I could not bear to think of it, or of the suffering which lay ahead. I could not bear it, and I did not—at least for the first two days I was in bed with the flu. Perhaps it was just as well—it wasn't the time to do any serious thinking. But once I was rested, I *had* to think of it, for most of the happiness and welfare of the four people I loved best in all the world lay in my hands. What I thought and said and felt and did in these next months would make it harder or easier for Jim, and would mold my children's future. *"Oh, God, give me wisdom. Help me to be strong and of good courage."*

Jim and I had always talked so freely, I don't know why we didn't mention his death then. I felt sure he knew, but I didn't want to be the first to say anything about it. I was hurting so badly with the knowledge of its coming, I was afraid I couldn't speak of it without choking over the words, while I knew I could *seem* calm if *he* spoke first.

If I had not been in bed with flu that first Sunday we were home again, I would have known. Later I found listed carefully in his handwriting in the pastoral record book the topic for that morning: "On Death."

He might just as well have preached a sermon "On Courage," for that was the sermon he now lived. He had been away from Princeton just three weeks—had missed only two Sundays from his pulpit.

By the world's standards, his every expectation had changed in that time. He knew he was doomed to die; his dream of twenty years of service before retirement was not to be realized. He had been ordained only a year and a half, had served in this church only a year, and half of that had been divided between the church and his studies at seminary. There was for him very little time.

But Jim turned his back on the judgments of the world when he set his feet on this path, and for him nothing had changed. His life was in God's hands still. He had been given a warning of the limitation of time, but he had always known death must come to every man.

At that time, only he, I, and the doctors knew he was a dying man. While the sentence was not immediate, we knew it was final. But if time was running out, he must make it count, make it count. He had no wish to be dramatic, so he did not make this known to his people—but he wanted them to understand clearly the teaching on death, so that when his time came, they might remember his words. He had begun his reading from Paul's first letter to the Corinthians.

"I would remind you, brethen, in what terms I preached to you the gospel, which you received, in which you stand, by which you are saved, if you hold it fast ... By the grace of God I am what I am, and his grace toward me was not in vain ... As in Adam all die, so also in Christ shall all be made alive ... (Christ) must reign until he has put all his enemies under his feet. The last enemy to be destroyed is death ... Then shall come to pass the saying that is written: 'Death is swallowed up in victory. . . .'

"Therefore, my beloved brethren, be steadfast, immovable, always abounding in the work of the Lord, knowing that in the Lord your labor is not in vain."

Death to Jim was nothing to be dreaded, but a victory, moving the believer from this world into a more wonderful realm: "In Christ shall all be made alive." Until it came to him, he was content to follow the admonition: he would be steadfast, immovable, abounding in the work of the Lord, knowing that his labor was not in vain.

I had heard it said you can get used to anything, but until this siege, I hadn't really believed it. It *is* surprising, though, just how much you *can* get used to, how adaptable the human mind and body are. For years I had worked with Jim's diabetes, planning his diet, running tests for sugar and giving him the necessary shots of insulin each day. When he traveled, he did these things for himself, but when I was with him I always tried to spare him the endless nuisance.

To this routine, we gradually added more and more. Jim no longer rested well, but was often up in the night. When he began to cough, he just got worse and worse, until he was tempted to sit up all night after a coughing spell. I am such a heavy sleeper that it is almost impossible for me to awaken once I have gone to sleep. Then, though, I learned I *could* wake up, and that if I would massage Jim as soon as he began to cough, I could get him relaxed enough to go back to sleep again, and so give him a little more strength for the next day. But I had my rewards. As I struggled up from slumber to work on him and give him rest, he would mumble as he drifted off to sleep, "Jane, I love you."

"Yes, I know, dear. Just call me Friday." And I rubbed on.

It was very clear, though, that Jim was making no gain, because he quickly needed more blood. In Princeton, there was no Blood Bank, so I had to find a donor with "type A positive" blood each time Jim needed a transfusion.

Bernice Davis, our wonderful organist, had come by when I was first wondering how to go about getting blood, and she and my friend Betsy Morgan proved my best sources of donors. Several men in our own church had the right type: Bill Woolwine, a Sunday school teacher, George Eldred, the church treasurer, and others. Reg Lowery, the husband of one of our members, gave blood, and found some fellow workers from the telephone company who would also give. Some people came voluntarily—but I had to ask most of the donors.

You can ask your friends for almost anything but their blood. When it comes to that, you never know when you are straining a friendship beyond the breaking point. The more I had to ask for blood, the more difficult it was for me.

It came to a point when my hands would get clammy with perspiration when Ralph would say we needed more blood, and I would go over in my mind all the possibilities, all those I knew who had the right blood type, or might possibly have. Then I would eliminate those I knew were sickly, those who had given blood recently, those I thought it would embarrass too much to ask—until I finally decided on two or three, hoping one of that list would be able and willing to give.

I soon learned all the excuses people can make for not giving blood. I hope I learned the proper face-saving replies for those who could not or would not give. I tried my best to look understanding and sympathetic when a great strapping hulk of a man began to explain why he could not give. After all, I'm a great big strapping hulk of a woman myself, and I cannot give blood without risk of also giving the most serious form of hepatitis with it, so I could never judge another person.

Despite the disappointments I encountered, the roll of those who gave blood for Jim grew ever longer, overwhelmingly so. Mary Wilson Eldred gave a pint, and laughingly began to call Jim "Cousin," as she said they were now "blood kin."

Jim loved the little joke, and called her "Cousin Mary Wilson" in return.

He became "cousin" to at least two people a month, and to each he owed a gift of life. With each transfusion his color would become ruddy and natural again, his steps springier, his reactions and abilities more normal. Then in ten days or so, he would be slowed down again, pale, with swollen feet and legs, and only his tremendous will could move his heavy body.

He was absolutely determined not to give in to his illness as long as he could put one foot before another. He would still walk the two blocks to the church as often as possible, sometimes stopping every few feet along the way to greet people. People automatically gravitated toward him. This had always been true of him, but it somehow seemed as if his suffering increased his magnetism.

There were times when he was in such pain that he seemed to see no one, but it was rare for him not to be alert to every opportunity to speak to others, no matter how he was feeling.

Because he refused to surrender or even admit his growing weakness, Jim was still besieged by heavy demands on his time and energies. I did what I could to lighten his burdens, but there seemed so little I could do.

In the fall, Jim had invited the ministers of each church in town to bring their wives to our house for dessert and an evening of fellowship. The group proved to be so congenial and so much fun, that for a time we met each month in the home of one of the group.

The men also began to meet once a month at lunch to discuss mutual problems the churches faced, ways of working together, and of helping the members of different churches to understand one another in spite of differences which would always remain. As fellowship and mutual liking grew among this group of men, their influence showed in small ways.

Jim suggested the group sponsor a leadership-training course, using the courses outlined and accredited by the National Council of Churches. This would help to train leaders for the individual churches—but by pooling their efforts they could provide training of a higher calibre than any one church could manage alone.

The school had been scheduled for early in February, and Jim had the job of organizing and getting it accredited. Fortunately he had done all the preliminary work before he got sick. But a few days before the school was to begin, the leader he had secured to teach the course on leading junior high groups had notified Jim he would be unable to come.

Jim telephoned frantically to find a leader for the course—but it was too late to secure someone from out of town to teach it. The day before the school began, he said, "Jane, there is no help for it. I'm going to have to teach that course. I might as well spend the rest of my time in preparation."

"Jim, you can't. You aren't strong enough to do that now."

Simple protest wouldn't be enough to move him, I knew. I had to suggest some alternative, and the only one I had was me. Despite the fact that I *hate* teaching adults, since I always feel they know more than I do, I said as firmly as I could, "You just can't do it. You owe your first loyalty—and strength—to your own church. I'll teach the course for you."

"Oh, baby, would you? I know you can do it."

I was stuck with it. I knew it would take all the nerve I had to stand up every night and tell fifteen people how to do jobs they were already doing, but if I didn't, Jim would. He could do it far better, but it was more than apparent he should not. The class would have to bear with my ineptness.

They were a gracious and understanding group. Although my stomach rose up within me and turned over with a butterfly sensation before each session, I managed to get through all ten sessions with a fair amount of self-possession, and the group were so anxious to help me that discussions were prompt and fruitful. Everyone tried to contribute to the class to put me more at ease, so it proved to be in many ways satisfying.

The entire school was successful, and so enthusiastically received that all the churches wanted to make it an annual affair; plans were laid then to continue. Jim had been unable to come to the meetings at all, and the Methodist minister had taken over the leadership.

On the third day of March Betsy called to say Reg and Robbie Lou Lowery's little girl was in the hospital. Sarah Jane was only two and a half, and had fallen against the door handle of the car as her mother was turning out into the street from their driveway. She had fallen on her head and suffered a concussion and a fractured skull.

It was one of Jim's bad days, but he insisted on getting up out of bed and going out to the hospital as soon as he heard the news. Sarah Jane's hospital room was dim, and she lay flat on her back in a little crib, with sandbags piled carefully around her head to keep it immobile. Her usually rosy, round face was ashen, and she looked terribly small and frail and helpless. Robbie Lou stood with her hands on the side of the crib, looking down at her child. She looked up with relief when we came. Any company at such a time is a helpful distraction, and Robbie Lou was still waiting for the results of the X rays. She told us they would really know nothing until Sarah Jane regained consciousness. Reg was working out of town and had not yet heard.

There was nothing we could do to help Sarah Jane except to pray. Jim took Robbie Lou's hand in his, laid his other hand on Sarah Jane's tiny body, and began softly to pray, committing Sarah Jane and her mother to the will of God. Most times, you must simply wait for an answer to prayer, but this time, when Jim finished, and raised his head, I was sure the answer would be what we hoped.

Robbie Lou felt the same assurance, for as she raised her head, though there were tears of deep emotion in her eyes, she had a glow of confidence and composure. Sarah Jane turned restlessly under Jim's hand, and we three smiled at one another like conspirators as we turned to leave.

Perhaps Jim shouldn't have gone. He was exhausted when we got home again, and after he had painfully gotten into the house, he dropped on the bed without even taking off his clothes. Perhaps he should have hoarded his energy—but to what purpose? The disease which was destroying him would run its course in any case. I was selfish enough to wish I could keep him with me longer—but I could only admire him for being willing to pour out for others what little he still had of life.

Although my thoughts and consciousness were very much centered on Jim's illness, his concern seemed to be only how he could best keep it from interfering with his work. He managed so well; life on the surface remained much the same. Yet his strength varied greatly from one day to the next. When he had to miss several Sundays in a row, he began to think he was not being fair to the church in trying to go on when he never knew whether or not he could preach, and when he could not make all the calls he should be making.

On a Sunday late in April, he invited the session down to the manse for its regular monthly meeting and asked me to have a special dessert ready for them when they came. I fixed hot coffee and pie, and excused myself after serving them.

After the meeting, Jim came in to lie down. The morning church service and then the meeting had drained his strength. I began to massage his back and legs, hoping he could relax enough to nap before the evening service. While I worked, he told me about the meeting.

"Jane, I went in there with every intention of resigning. I told them I couldn't do the job I came here to do, that I would very probably have to rest for the next few months. Well, I just never got to state clearly that I was resigning. They began to reassure me—I could take all the time I wanted if I needed rest, they could make arrangements, I was still of use to the church even if I was ill. . . . They felt the people were united, they were certainly working and enthusiastic, in fact someone said it might just be a good thing for more of the members to take some of the responsibility of the church on their shoulders.

"I declare, Jane, I feel it isn't right to stay on if I can't work —though I had hoped to see this building through. I don't know whether I should stay or not." But I knew he really wanted to stay—and neither of us really believed he could live more than a few months. If he could be useful here, it would be good for us to stay on. I was pleased with the session for being so generous, for I felt they had been obtuse on purpose.

I was more convinced by the end of the afternoon, for after the men had gone to their homes and told their wives of Jim's readiness to resign, the word traveled around the community. To our amazement, small groups of people dropped in all afternoon, two or three or four at at time.

"Mr. Huff," one would finally say, "we just came to ask you not to think any more about leaving. Even if you cannot preach, even if you have to stay in bed all the time, you are doing us more good just being here than you can know."

The people of Princeton had shown us a warm and generous spirit from the time of our coming. Now, their love became even more apparent, and was a heart-warming thing. As I walked about the streets of the little town, strangers stopped me, just to say a word, to ask about Jim, in some way to say their thoughts were with us. Casual acquaintances paused to make themselves known, to share their sympathy. In the four months of Jim's illness, many who had not especially thought about us before began to identify themselves with us and to us:

"I've never met you, but I feel I know you well. A friend of mine has told me so much about you, and I just had to stop to say how much I admire your husband. We have never seen anything like him. . . . "

Another said, "It is so seldom that a really big man chooses to stay in a small town. . . ."

Everywhere I went, people spoke to me, rejoicing that our

session had been so generous that they wanted Jim to stay whatever the circumstances.

"You belong to us," said one. "We cannot let you go."

It was an amazing demonstration, and was to grow as the months went by. How kind people were—and how much Jim must have affected the community in so little time!

White had suggested Jim return for a check up in April, so I drove Jim over to Chattanooga. White ran the usual battery of tests, then shook his head over the results. "You might be only forty-seven, and think you are still a young man," he told Jim frankly, "but your body is that of a man in his late sixties. You have burned yourself out."

The first time Jim's illness made itself apparent to his parishioners I was not there to give him my support. In the spring Jim's health and strength had seemed to improve with the weather, and I yielded to his suggestion that I take the children on a brief vacation to visit my mother when school was out.

We were hardly gone a week when I received word through friends that Jim had been taken ill during service on Sunday. I immediately headed home. I couldn't stay in Florida if Jim was sick—and the children had seen their grandmother, and the ocean. When we arrived, Jim was painfully embarrassed that we had come and rather noncommittal about how sick he had been.

It was from "Cousin" Mary Wilson Eldred I learned the story. In the pulpit that Sunday morning, Jim had announced the sermon topic, then opened the big pulpit Bible to read the Scripture lesson. But instead of his usual firm delivery, he read haltingly, as if he did not quite grasp the words. He finished reading, and stood for a moment, leaning against the pulpit, then began to pray, so softly no one could hear him.

George Eldred, sitting in the choir, knew something was wrong, and finally felt he should do something about it. He hated to make himself conspicuous during a service, but some-

one had to do something—the service was becoming a mock-
ery. When Jim announced a hymn, Bernice began to play and
Olive Eldred led the choir in singing, while George slipped out
the rear and came round the side to the pulpit.

George, always a gentleman, was courteous and tactful.
"Jim," he said cautiously, "I'm afraid you aren't feeling well.
Don't try to preach for us this morning." He might as well
have waved a red flag before a bull, for Jim would never let
a little thing like not feeling well stop him from preaching.

If George had been blunt and had said something like, "Jim,
you sound like hell this morning, don't try to preach," he might
have been more successful. As it was, Jim had his sermon well
prepared, and he was going to give it. George, seeing no alternative other than removing him bodily from the pulpit, hoped
it wouldn't be as bad as he had feared, and returned to the
choir.

Everyone in the congregation was by now thoroughly
alarmed, but each one was trying to preserve an appearance
of normality so as to keep the worship service going as usual.
When the hymn ended, Jim stood unsteadily, then reeled and
staggered drunkenly toward the pulpit. No one knew how to
stop him. No one quite dared to interrupt the service to tell him
it was wrong, that he was not really preaching at all, so he stood
in the pulpit, and tried to go through the motions of preaching
the sermon he had prepared.

As Mary Wilson told it, my heart ached for all those who had
to sit helplessly and watch. I was hurt for Jim, trying so desperately to serve out of the love of his heart, going through the
ignominy of that service.

He had managed to finish, but with an agony of effort. Yet
he was incoherent—and no eye in the congregation was dry.
What was happening to him, no one knew; that something was
happening, there was no doubt.

At last the agony was over. Jim closed the service with a
benediction and stumbled to his seat, aware he was very ill.

Everyone rushed forward to help him. He wanted to go home, and someone took him, while someone else went to the Methodist church to summon Ralph Cash out of service to come to Jim.

The reason for his illness was entirely an anticlimax: after twenty-five years as a diabetic, Jim had for the first time in his life had an insulin reaction. As soon as he was given some sugar, he snapped back to normal. Later, he figured out why he had had the reaction.

"I gave myself my usual injection of insulin," he said. "Then, it was such a beautiful morning that I walked while I went over my sermon. I felt fine during Sunday school, but during the last part of the service, I began to realize something was wrong. If I had just known what it was, I had some lump sugar in my pocket—but I don't remember any of the usual warning signs. I was just sick."

We had come home on a false alarm—all Jim had needed was a lump of sugar. Nevertheless, I could understand the concern of our people, and how shattering an experience it must have been for them. I made up my mind never again to be absent from any service at which he was to preach.

Shortly after, we heard that our close friend at seminary, Jim Thorn, had caught pneumonia doing rescue work during the late spring floods of the Ohio River. Jim wrote at once to Jim Thorn and had a prompt and cheerful reply, full of news and hope. He was over the worst of his illness, he wrote, and had expected to be at home already, but some minor setback had kept him in the hospital. Meanwhile, his son was looking toward his first birthday in June, and they were expecting their second child late in July. "It's been a good year for us," he concluded cheerfully. "Hard to realize it's still been less than a year since graduation, Joe's birth, my ordination—we've had so many wonderful experiences this last year. Things have really been happening to Father Thorn. I guess this last experience has been to help me in my ministry to the sick. See you at Synod in July."

Jim was resting after the morning service on the fifth of June when a friend called to tell us Jim Thorn had died that morning, about an hour before his wife was to have taken him home from the hospital.

"Oh, no," I protested foolishly. "Noma hasn't even had her baby yet, has she?"

"No," he answered. "It isn't due for another month."

"I'm so sorry! We loved Jim beyond measure. We had planned to see them and little Joe when we came over for Synod, though Jim will be lucky if he gets to Synod—he's been worse the last few days. Jim's going to want to come to Noma now, but I don't think he's strong enough to ride three hundred miles. Please tell Noma we care, and explain why Jim doesn't come."

Jim wanted to go, but knew as well as I he should not. That night at the evening service, he spoke of Jim Thorn's death:

My best friend at seminary died this morning. Jim Thorn was only thirty, with all of life's opportunity before him. He was ordained a little less than a year ago, and went to serve in Augusta, a little community in the northeast part of the state. This spring in the flooding Ohio, he worked too long trying to rescue others who were trapped in the waters, and caught pneumonia. He was apparently almost well again—ready to leave the hospital—when he died quite suddenly this morning.

Jim's training was long and hard earned, yet I feel sure he would have gone on with it even if he had known how limited his service was to be, for he was a joyous and vital Christian, thoroughly committed to the will of God for his life, ready for his ministry to be used as God saw fit. Even a short service can have great worth, for it is after all the quality of his service, rather than its length which gives the measure of a man.

We do not understand why one man is called by death and

another allowed to remain. We leave that in the hands of God. But Jim was happy in his ministry, and I believe God used his buoyant spirit to change some life.

Even while Jim Huff paid tribute to his friend, it seemed he was summarizing his own views of the ministry. As he said even a short service was worthwhile, he seemed to tell us that he, too, was reconciled to a short service. He, too, was happy in his ministry, and he left it to God to use as He saw fit.

In June, Ralph took his brief annual vacation to attend a medical meeting in Chicago. He checked Jim quite thoroughly before he left, gave him a transfusion, and left us supplies and instructions for all we were likely to need during his absence.

Jim, however, didn't follow his usual pattern. By the end of the week he was much worse. He looked bad. His legs were swollen more than they ever had been; they looked grotesque over the tops of shoes which he could barely manage to lace. His body was heavy, his face looked drawn and haggard, and I didn't see how he could preach. Yet, no matter how burdensome his body was, his mind and spirit never faltered, and he wanted to go on.

I went to his study to check on him just before Sunday morning service. He looked so bad I left quickly, not wanting him to see how it upset me. When I glanced back, he had started slowly out of the study, walking with dragging steps down the hall, while I went the other way to the back of the church.

Bernice, our organist, said she watched Jim drag himself up the four steps to the choir room. He stood with the choir, chatting quietly, then nodded to Bernice as she walked toward the organ. As she passed him, she said softly, "You look tired."

"So tired," he answered sadly. "So very, very tired."

Bernice watched him as she played the prelude. He leaned against the wall, apart from the others, as if he were unable to stand alone. Then he closed his eyes, as if in prayer, and finally straightened up, as if a load had been lifted from his shoulders.

The lines seemed to drop from his face, and as he led the choir in, he smiled ruefully at Bernice as she played the processional.

In my pew, I was amazed, as I was to be so often, at the change in Jim. He could draw on the hidden reserves of the spirit as another man could draw money from the bank. It made me think of the little Gospel hymn, "There is power, power, power in the blood. . . ." It certainly took power to do what he was doing.

But the power was short lived. By the end of the service, it was apparent he was exhausted, and before the benediction he paused to ask the session to come to the front of the church for a short meeting.

He sat down in his pulpit chair, not even attempting to go down and greet people as they left the church. When the session gathered, he said simply, "I seem to have gone beyond my strength; I want to ask to be excused from conducting the evening service tonight."

They voted to excuse him. After thanking them, Jim said wryly, "If I had any sense, I'd be on my way to Chattanooga to see White, since Ralph is out of town."

Dick Morgan immediately sensed how important the remark was. He suggested to Betsy that they take the children if I could get Jim to go. Betsy came to find me while Jim went to his study to take off his robe, and due to the kindness of these friends the matter was quickly arranged.

I left at once, to have Jim's lunch ready and his bag packed before he got home. When he came, everything was ready. "Jim, I'm going to take you to Chattanooga as soon as you've eaten. Everything is packed," I went on hastily, "and the children are cared for."

"What?" he asked in astonishment. "How did you get that idea?"

"Well, you told the session you should see White, and Dick thought you should too, so everything is arranged. I'll take you as soon as you eat."

"But, Jane," he protested, "I have meetings with the sessions of the Crane and Francis churches at three and three-thirty. The meetings shouldn't take too long—but they're a good twenty miles from here."

"Well, that's all right," I said. "We'll go to your meetings. As soon as they are over, we'll have the suitcases in the car, and can go straight to Chattanooga."

That was what we did. The meetings were time consuming, though, and when, finally, we left for Chattanooga, it was four-fifteen. It was midnight when we arrived. "Jane," Jim said, "let's stop at a motel and phone White before we go on."

I did as he asked, but it was he who phoned White. Being Jim, when he found that White was already in bed, he gave no hint of why we had come to Chattanooga, but just said we would see him in the morning.

By morning, it was evident that I had been most unwise. I should not have stopped to make that phone call. Jim was sicker this morning than he had ever been.

When White saw him, once again he called for a room at the hospital. "Cotton, why on earth didn't you tell me last night you were this sick? You made it sound like you'd come over for a social visit!"

Weak as he was, Jim could still grin. "Well, I never like to admit I'm sick, and it was midnight. I couldn't see it was worth your while to stay up for me."

"If you'd waited much longer, you wouldn't have had any more mornings."

I took Jim out to the hospital. While I registered him, a nurse took him up to his room. By the time I finished in the office, he was in bed in his pajamas, and the first of a relay of teams was in his room, beginning a lengthy series of tests, and getting started on the transfusions.

"Come on in, baby," he called when he saw me at the door.

"They're taking blood out of one arm and putting it in the other."

With rollicking good humor, he entertained the nurses and interns who came in to minister to him. Typically, he learned something about each one and found some common topic of conversation.

I was determined not to rebel at what was happening to Jim —but I couldn't take it as lightly as he seemed to! I couldn't laugh and be as gay as he was.

I talked privately to White. "Is this the time," I asked him bluntly, "or will he get on his feet again? This looks very bad to me."

"Oh, you got here in time. He definitely needed hospitalization, and we'll get him on his feet again, but this will happen again until there comes a time when nothing will help."

There had been a particular horror in watching Jim the last few days. He had grown so much worse so quickly, and the change in the twenty-four hours before we got to the hospital had been dismaying. The knowledge that it could happen again and again in just this way was almost more than I could bear.

"God give me grace to see him through it," I prayed, and went back to Jim's room to do what I could for him.

The next morning, I went to the hospital immediately after breakfast. Jim was beginning to show signs of responding to the treatment White had prescribed, and looked much better.

That afternoon, a telegram came from Lois and Richard Ratliff in Princeton: "Instead of sending flowers, we are putting $100 in the fund for landscaping Huff Court. With all love."

This was followed by others, until Jim was beaming. "Wasn't that a smart thing to do? I'd been wondering how we were going to do anything with that spot. It ought to be a real beauty spot by the time we dedicate the new building."

Nothing could have pleased Jim more.

There was another worry on my mind at this time. As we had feared, John's first eye operation had not completely solved the problem of his split vision, and he was already scheduled to undergo surgery a second time. This operation was to take place just over a week after the day Jim arrived at the hospital. As the days passed, I grew more and more anxious about it. Finally, on Saturday, I said to Jim, "Would it be better to put it off so I can stay here with you?"

"No, Jane," he said firmly. "If the date is set, it will be better for John to have it and be done with it. It might be that this is the last one for him. So much the better for him if it is . . . but if we put it off, and I should die in a hospital before he has his operation, it might make him afraid to go, and it's enough of an ordeal for the child without adding to his fears. If you're up to it, go on and take him. I just wish you didn't have to do it all alone."

We arranged, then, that Claire would again do the visiting with Jim, and I would leave the next day for Princeton. Early Sunday morning, I said goodbye to Jim and set out for home.

Physically, I knew I was walking the edge of a precipice, but it never worried me, for I felt God was guiding me, and I counted on Him to give me the strength for every task—"As thy days, so shall thy strength be." For once, I was not trying to plan everything out, but just taking one step at a time in faith. I suppose if I had ever looked down into the abyss of trouble awaiting us if my strength failed, I might have fallen into it. Instead, as I look back now, I can see it was not the possibility of a fall that mattered, but the fact that from the height I saw life in a new dimension. I had a sense of God's strength and presence which put both joy and peace in my heart.

We have no language to describe the experiences of the spirit. Paul prayed the Ephesians might have Christ dwelling in their hearts, and so grow in love they might understand "the breadth and length and height and depth" of it. Perhaps that is as close as we can come. We really do not have in our language the words to explain to one another the new awareness of life, the deepening and enrichment of all life's experiences which are a part of a growing Christian faith.

I arrived late in the afternoon. The girls were thrilled to see me. Poor John was not, because he knew why I had come home. I collected all the children's belongings and got them all settled in at home. John's hostess, Elizabeth Woolwine, had very generously laundered all his pajamas so he was ready to go to the hospital; next morning I had only to pack his suitcase and start.

As I drove John to Nashville, he turned to me. "Mother," he said earnestly, "I don't *want* to go!"

I thought how dreadfully ill ether always made him, how terror engulfed him when the anesthetist put the cone over his face, and how he fought it, violently, and awakened from it still fighting. "No, son," I tried to reassure him, "of course you don't want to go. It's a hard thing to do. But still all of us have to go through some disagreeable things in life. We can't always see why at the time, we often just have to trust God to give us the strength to go through it, and the wisdom to learn something from it. At least it won't take long. By this time tomorrow, it will be over, and you will be waking up. You won't feel very nice until the next day, but after that, it will be just the blindfold for a week, then you'll be able to see so much better for all the rest of your life."

"I know, Mom. But I *still* don't want to go."

I didn't blame him in the least.

The day of the operation was terrible for him. But the next morning, he seemed much better. I was only allowed to visit him for an hour, and then was told we would have to observe regular visiting hours for the wing: from two-thirty to three-thirty in the afternoon, and from seven to eight in the evening. Since I was to be so very limited in the time I could spend with John, I decided to go back to Jim.

Of course, I couldn't have left if it would have upset John. But he was in a room with three other children, who had all come in on Monday afternoon. They had shared the same tests and fears. All had undergone surgery on Tuesday. By now they were comrades of long standing. When I asked John how he would feel if I went back to his daddy, he said, "Oh, heck, Mom. Go ahead. We're having fun."

Middle-sized boys only need mothers in emergencies, and now the emergency was over for John. He was content at my leaving. In fact he seemed a little glad to get rid of me.

I reached the hospital in Chattanooga just after supper. The look on Jim's face, when he caught sight of me, was enough to make the long drive worthwhile. Words would have been superfluous. He just grinned and asked, "How was John when you left him?"

"As far as I could tell, he was delighted to see me go so he and the boy on the next bed could get on with their cowboy and Indian game!"

On Friday, White told us Jim could go home the next day. "But don't think you're going home on Saturday and preach on Sunday," he warned. "You're not as strong as you think, even if you *can* walk from that bed to the chair and back again. If you expect to do any more preaching, give yourself time to get back on your feet before you do it."

On Saturday we went home. Jim was relieved to be back. It was a relief for me, too, to have Jim home again and to know John would be back in a few days. It was going to be mighty good to have all of us in the same spot at once.

In the July sun, the house was stifling. Jim wandered about, lumberingly on heavy feet.

Our bedroom seemed to be the hottest room downstairs. While it was pleasant enough in the early morning, it soon grew hot and airless, and was quite impossible by afternoon. Jim rarely stayed there. He could not climb the stairs to his study, and so paced through the house like an injured elephant looking for some place cool enough to be comfortable.

Finally, I put two chairs out between two oak trees near the sidewalk, where there was a fairly deep shade, and we took to sitting outside. It was pleasant there. Our street was the only one that ran to the south end of town from the square, so a great many people passed by. Most of them stopped to chat.

The square was a fairly high piece of ground, which began to slope gently down toward us. Across the street from the manse, and down the alley a bit, there was a sharp drop, which led into an extremely poor section, known generally as "Black Bottom." Here lived the discouraged, the defeated, those who had wrested nothing from life and barely existed on the fringe of it, hungry in body and soul for the food and the beauty that seemed to lie always beyond their reach. They dwelt in shanties for the most part, shacks hastily and carelessly built, which defiantly held together to give shelter to those who lived in them. But it was a mean shelter, too hot in summer, too cold in winter, leaving the occupants forever at the mercy of the weather.

There had been several desultory attempts to buy up the land, tear down the shacks, clear the rubbish and dirt from the little stream running through the Bottom, and build a public park with a swimming pool. But the attempts had been too haphazard. There were never enough people of means and influence ready to back the project or to give up their income from the property, so it died from lack of interest, and the Bottom continued as it had always been, an abscess just below sight of the town, but always painfully there.

As Jim and I sat under the trees, savoring at least the thought of coolness and enjoying each other's company, a middle-aged woman came toiling up the alley from the Bottom. Her feet made little puffs of dust each time she set them down on the bone-dry earth of the alley, and in the heat, the exertion of the short climb had beaded her face with sweat. Her face had the slack, weary expression of those who have found life too much to bear and have resigned themselves to just getting through it, one foot before the other, just as she was now making her way up the alley.

She reached the street and stood for a moment, a little breathless, glancing casually up and down for cars, then starting across. When she reached our side, she saw Jim, and her expression changed. Reaching back for some almost forgotten respectability, she straightened, wiped at the perspiration on her face and brushed at her graying hair.

"Well, preacher," she said. "I heard you was awfully sick."

"That's what they told me, but I don't give up too easily."

I had gotten up when she came to stand by us, and Jim introduced us. She looked so miserably hot, I asked, "Won't you sit down? I'll go get us some lemonade."

Pleased, she sat. "My relief check come, I was goin' up to buy some groceries."

When I came back with a pitcher of lemonade on a tray, I poured her a tall glass, and just a scant half glass for Jim because he could only have a limited amount of liquid. Then I went back to get another chair so I could sit with them. We talked pleasantly in the shade of the trees, savoring the cold, sweet drink. When it was gone, the woman rose, reluctantly, to go on to town and her errand. "My, that was good," she said as she left us.

"A cup of cold water," said Jim softly, after she had walked out of earshot. Her step seemed springier, more purposeful as she moved on up the street.

"Who was she, Jim? How did you happen to know her?"

"She came to my office last winter. She'd been sick, and so had her teen-age daughter. She had gone to a Presbyterian church once somewhere—and just decided maybe we could help her. She had been deserted by her husband and had been trying to make a decent living for her daughter, but a series of small misfortunes had gotten her down. I asked Mrs. Ingram and Mrs. Towery to find them some warm clothes, found she was eligible for relief, and showed her how to apply for it. She comes by to talk every once in a while."

"Can you do anything more to help her?"

"I've been thinking about it, baby, but so far I haven't found any solution. She's not strong enough to do regular work, and she has gotten beyond the point where she would even be willing to take on any regular responsibilities. I guess she needs friends more than anything else. Why don't you take time next week to walk down and call on her?"

"I'll try, honey, after I get John home and settled again."

It was only a few minutes before Frank Craig stopped by. Frank was an elder in the church, a tall, raw-boned man, mild and gentle, anxious to please yet hesitant lest he be in the way. He was big-hearted and shy, and completely devoted to his wife Louisa. Louisa was a teacher, and had also taught many years in Sunday school. She was loved by everyone. She was just as much in love with Frank as she must have been when she first married him. Louisa had been ill all spring, and had recently undergone surgery which revealed a malignancy. We were all deeply concerned about her.

Just now, Frank was terribly discouraged. He tried not to show it as he greeted Jim in his shy way. "We're mighty glad you're back home again, Mr. Huff."

"It's good to come home again, Frank. How is Louisa?"

Frank gave a brief impatient shake of his head which said more than words could have. "Oh, she's not feeling too well. Sent you her regards."

"Tell her I'll be down to see her tomorrow or the next day."

"Oh, Mr. Huff, there's no call for you to come down," he protested. "Louisa knows you've been sick."

"Well, Frank, if I can walk this far," Jim said, "I can walk a few steps farther to the car, and Miss Jane can drive me down. I want to see Louisa, so I'll be down in a day or so."

"She'd be mighty pleased to see you. She thinks a lot of you, Mr. Huff."

People, people, people. So began what Dr. Caldwell named Jim's "rocking chair ministry." Now that he was too ill to seek out others, they came to him—and it was a measure of the man that many came. The chairs emptied and were filled again.

Almost anyone else would have sought a secluded spot for convalescence—but not Jim. He wanted to be where he could see and hear and feel the pulse of the town, so here he sat in front of the house. Ill he might be, and weak in body—but there was no failing of the spirit of love for his fellow man, nor any failing of his keen gifts of mind. With an opportunity to use these gifts, he lost his feeling of caged restlessness and was willing to sit through the days here.

On Wednesday, I went down for John. He met me with the happy enthusiasm of a pup which has been penned up for weeks. He was wild with excitement, glad to be getting out of the hospital, glad to be going home, and hoping there would never be another operation. He talked all the way home without pause. We celebrated his homecoming with his favorite meal, topped with ice cream and cake and small family foolishness.

On his second Sunday at home, Jim returned to his pulpit. Still, he was not strong enough to do much more than preach. I drove him down to see Louisa, and to make a few other calls, but the greater part of his days were spent holding his levees under the oaks.

Jim's vacation was scheduled for August, and once more he demurred, saying he had been away too much. "Never mind about that, Jim. You know you need to be quiet a while longer, and you'll be better off on the mountain than here in the heat of August."

"I know I would," he admitted, "but it doesn't seem right."

He was uneasy about going until he had a note from his seminary classmate John D. Reese, who was back in the states
after his year of study in Italy, and looking for a church.

"Jane," Jim called to me happily, "I'm going to ask the
pulpit supply committee if they wouldn't like to have John
D. Reese come here for the month of August, and I'll pay his
salary. That way, they'll have a good man, and I won't feel
guilty about not serving the church. He knows the people here,
and he can do a lot of good."

The week before we were to leave, he told me Carl had just
stopped by, to say he wished to join the church.

"I almost told him I'd arrange for a special session meeting,
then receive him publicly at the church service on Sunday
before we leave for our vacation. But I was so surprised when
Carl told me, I said I would like to wait until September when
we return."

"But, Jim," I began, and then could not go on, for I hated
to say the rest of my thought: *"Suppose you don't come back
—that's almost six weeks away, and you don't know how
long . . ."* And as so often happened, Jim read my thought.

"I know, baby, I know. I might not come back at all—but
Carl took me by surprise, and it just seemed better to do it
properly, with a communicant's class beforehand, than to do
it hastily."

Jim was usually more discerning than I, and it was his
business. Also, if he did not come back, there would be someone else to receive Carl into the church—he was not a person
to turn aside once his mind was made up.

What, I wondered, had made him decide now? Carl had
been raised a Catholic, but married a Presbyterian. His wife
was a member of the church, his children had been baptized
there, and his son Bill was now clerk of the session. For more
than twenty years, Carl had been bringing his family and their
friends to the church, often worshiping there himself. His

interest had grown enormously in recent years, especially after he had taken on the chairmanship of the building committee, and he had worked hard on the new building.

Much later, when I had a chance to ask him, I couldn't resist the opportunity: "Carl, what made you decide just then?"

"I suppose I'd been coming to it for a long time," he said. "I'd felt I was neither fish nor fowl, for I wasn't active in my own church, and I really hadn't taken a stand in this one. I always felt my mother wouldn't like to see me change, so I didn't plan to do anything about it."

"Then Jim came. Before you moved down, he used to come out to eat with us on weekends. While Anne fixed dinner, Jim and I would talk. He certainly is a fine man. His experience makes you respect him, and he's easy to talk to. Then I liked working with him on the new building. He knew what he wanted, and he knew how to get it without treading on people's feelings in the process. But it was his illness that really made me think. Daily annoyances assume unnecessary proportions in the lives of most of us, but it isn't that way with Jim. Watching him give everything he had, and live in trust and patience during his sickness, made me decide it was time I took a stand, so I did."

"Let the redeemed of the Lord say so."

Our stay in Claire's cabin on the mountain above Rockwood was sweet and restful. If Jim had not been ill, it would have been an idyllic vacation. It was the only quiet one we ever took, and the second longest. After the intense, muggy, drought-ridden, dusty heat of Kentucky, the fresh coolness of the mountain was balm to body and soul. The cumulative effect of transfusions in late June and early July had put Jim into fairly good shape, so I was not overly concerned about him.

We still had a week of vacation left when John D. called Jim to tell him Louisa had died. The mountain phone connection was poor, so Jim was shouting to make himself heard far away in Kentucky: "John D., thanks for calling. You tell Frank I'll be home in time for the funeral. If possible, we'll get in about noon tomorrow. Jane can pack this afternoon. I'll have to go down to the doctor before I can get away, but we ought to be able to leave the first thing in the morning."

He hung up and turned to face me. "Well, I can see you heard that. Can you take me down the mountain to see Uncle George, then come back to pack and be ready to go in the morning?"

"Yes, I can—but *why* did they have to call you? You could have had another week of rest!"

If only they had not called! Selfishly, I wanted Jim to have a little more time in this quiet spot, a little more of the coolness before we returned to the heat of western Kentucky. But there was really no choice. Even though Frank had told John D. to tell Jim not to come, once he knew of Louisa's death, Jim felt he must go. If a minister is told, he must go—he can hardly choose to be apart from his people in any time of sorrow. "Comfort ye, comfort ye my people," was the old instruction to the prophet, and remains one of the prophet's duties to this day.

We had loved Louisa, and we might be of some comfort to Frank and his sister Mary if we returned. What else could we do?

Jim had to have a transfusion before we could leave, and Uncle George arranged it for the following morning. For some reason, it went badly. It seemed to exhaust Jim more than it helped him. We got a late start back to Princeton, and by the time we arrived, Jim was too worn out to go to the funeral parlor. He had to go straight in to bed, so I went in his place.

Frank was still there. He put out his hands toward me in a helpless woebegone gesture. I took them in my own in some attempt to reassure him.

"You all didn't need to come home, Miss Jane," he said apologetically. "I didn't mean for them to send for you. I didn't want Mr. Huff to make the long trip on my account."

I *had* minded that Jim's vacation was cut short. I had been disappointed that we had to come home early, and it had distressed me to take the trip after the incident of the morning. But now that I was here, looking into Frank's face, I saw how touched and pleased he was that we had come, and I saw Jim had been right to come.

"We loved Louisa, Frank, and Jim wanted to come on your account. I made him go to bed just now, but he will see you in the morning."

At two the next day, the funeral parlor was jammed. Because I was late, I had to sit in the anteroom. Extra chairs were brought in, filling every empty space, so there was no aisle or passage.

Bernice was at the organ, Jim and John D. shared in the simple service. The air conditioning was on, but the crush of people was oppressing. The woman in front of me was crying softly. The music and words flowed around me. . . .

From where I sat, I could not see him, but I could hear Jim's voice reading:

"From everlasting to everlasting, thou art God. . . .
The days of our years are threescore years and ten;
And if by reason of strength they be fourscore years,
Yet is their strength labour and sorrow;
For it is soon cut off, and we fly away. . . ."

PSALM 90

"For it is soon cut off. . . ." Yes, it is soon cut off. If not yesterday or today, then some soon tomorrow. While I knew the prayer of faith and hope which followed these lines, my mind now seized on them with bitterness. I tried to push the whole thought away from me. But oh, I thought, funerals are pagan, and I wished I could be out of this place. The chairs were too close about me; there was no passage left. I had to sit and hear Jim voice the words of comfort which were today no comfort at all.

When at last it was over, we rose. Then attendants abruptly snatched the chairs in order to clear the anteroom, and I escaped as quickly as I could.

My friend and our loyal parishioner, Elizabeth Woolwine, went through the door just as I did. I caught her hand. "Elizabeth, help me get away from here without having to talk to anyone." Gracious, understanding Elizabeth. There are some people to whom you don't have to explain, and Elizabeth is one. "That was my last funeral until I go to his," I told her when we left the crowd behind. "It was more than I could endure again, to hear him read that service and know the words would soon be read for him."

At home, alone, I prayed. *"God help me. Help me not to be so weak, not to give in to my feelings so easily."*

I was not exactly rebellious—or I told myself I was not—but, oh, how it hurt. I could understand how God was using us, I could be acquiescent, I could do what was necessary; but nothing, not even the love of God, could assuage the hurt. I could see in myself the child John had been that summer. He had understood the necessity for his operation, so that his eyes might be opened, be more useful to him—but oh, the surgery *did* hurt.

If our experience was to be used for the growth of compassion within us, or so the eyes of someone might be opened to the working of the love of God, so be it—but oh, it hurt.

I was shaking with the effort at self-control and knew I had to do something to use up all my unspent emotions. I got out bowls and flour to bake a pie for John D. and the children for supper. When that was in the oven, I made a special diabetic dessert for Jim. By the time the two men came home again, I had a big supper ready, and my emotions had simmered down to normal.

The course for junior-high leaders I had taught the preceding spring was so well received that I was asked to repeat it for another group that fall. Again, to help out and spare Jim, I agreed to teach it.

I think Jim rather enjoyed having an excuse to stay home with the children each evening. He told them stories, and together they even watched television, a rare treat for Jim as well as the children.

It was a good course, and once again I had a loving and sympathetic class. However, the schedule was demanding, and I must have grown more tired than I realized. On the last night, I listened to Earl Caldwell, a young minister who had also been at Louisville seminary, discuss with his class the letters of Paul. He referred briefly to that well-known and well-loved sermon by Dr. Macartney of Pittsburgh, based on Paul's admonition: "Do your best to come before winter. . . ." I knew the sermon, and I also knew the letter in which Paul asked his disciple to bring his cloak and to come before winter, before the cold weather came, and while he would still have need of it, for he was at the close of his service and might have no more time left. Dr. Macartney had taken the phrase and built around it the warning that we are all approaching winter, that today will never come again, and unless we do today what we can, what is important, we may well never have another chance.

At home, Jim sat cheerfully with the children, but his winter was fast approaching.

Why, I thought, why? Why did it have to be Jim? Why couldn't he have had more time? Why? I loved him so much. I didn't want to give him up. I didn't want to watch the coming of winter. Nor did I want to see him suffer any more. Oh, God, why?

Lost in my own anguish, I was no longer listening to Earl. Silently, I began to pray for strength: *"God, I know we are in Your hands. Give me patience and understanding. Help me be willing to see it through . . . not my will, oh Lord, but Thine."*

To my shame, the tears came at last. Since January, I had known Jim's sentence had been passed. Tonight, betrayed by a word, caught unaware and unprepared, I had looked down the path ahead of me—wherein I must give up my love, part with that joyous and delightful spirit. . . . I could not contain my sorrow.

As always, I was sitting in the front row, so there was no easy way out. I sat alone, trying to compose myself, trying to turn my thoughts in another direction. I hoped no one but Earl could see me or realize what was happening to me. At last, during the closing prayer, I was able to slip out under cover of silence and the bowed heads of the congregation, and go to my car to be alone for a few minutes, to try to compose myself enough to teach during the next session.

I would have liked to run home, but that would have been cowardly, and if I did go home early, how would I explain to Jim? I had to stay. When I thought I had myself in hand, I went back into the church. There was no way to hide my tear-reddened eyes, but people were kind and no doubt understood.

A few days of crisp weather were followed by a perfect Indian-summer day. John brought home a notice from school about money for books, so I gave him the money in an envelope to take to his teacher, kissed him, and sent him off to school on his bicycle.

I got busy on the house cleaning and laundry, and Jim went to the church. As John's lunch period came at eleven-thirty, we decided we would all eat then, so I had lunch ready and waiting when Jim got home, but John did not come.

Finally, a little uneasy, I called the school to ask if he had stayed there for lunch. The principal sounded a bit embarrassed. "Mrs. Huff, I really intended to call you earlier. Some of the children said John was on the school grounds before school began, but he didn't come into class when the bell rang. One of the boys saw him ride off on his bicycle."

My heart sank. I had given him the book money, and it must have been a temptation to him.

We ate our lunch, worrying about John. I assumed he would come home about the usual time and pretend he had been in school . . . but three o'clock came, and John did not. The afternoon dragged on. Jim called a number of times, but John did not come. We tried to decide whether or not to call the police, but hated to do it.

"When he gets hungry, he'll come home," said Jim. "He certainly knows how to take care of himself. Just don't worry about him."

Now that was the sensible thing to do, just not worry about him. So we stopped talking about it, and each worried silently and added a silent prayer or two. "God, keep him out of trouble . . . let him be safe. . . ."

Jim tired quickly and this showed. He went to get ready for bed about eight, put on his pajamas, and stretched out on the bed. He was trying to be very calm about the whole thing.

At eight-fifteen, I said, "Jim, I can't stand it any longer. I have to call the police. Something must have happened to him."

"I know, honey, I just keep thinking if we wait a few minutes longer, he will come in. But you'd better call. Try Ed Johnstone; he's the juvenile judge in addition to his regular law practice. Ed can handle it for you."

I called Ed, who promised to try the local and state police. "I'll phone you as soon as we hear anything," he said.

I waited for an hour, until Jim warned me he might not be found that night. In a brave show of not worrying, I got ready for bed. We both lay still in the darkness, wondering where he had gone, what had happened to him.

At nine-thirty the phone rang. I snatched it eagerly. It was Ed, saying John was at Kentucky Lake—thirty miles away. He had eaten in the restaurant, paid for his supper, then asked the manager to phone a state trooper to take him home: he was too tired to ride thirty miles back on his bicycle!

Since the call for John had been put out an hour earlier, the trooper radioed in for instructions. "I'll go right down and get him," I told Ed.

"I'll be by for you in a few minutes," he said firmly and hung up before I could protest that I could go alone.

Jim insisted *he* should go, but I had dressed quickly, and I fussed at him, "No, you won't. I'll tend to our child. You save your strength for all those who still need you."

It must have been galling to have to let me go—but the doorbell rang, Ed was already at the door. I kissed Jim and helped him lift his heavy legs back onto the bed. "We'll be back before too long."

He waved me goodbye and laid himself wearily down again. "I love you, Jane." I knew he did—the words held love and resignation and tacit apology for not being able to go, but neither of us could have borne it if he had put it into words.

The thirty miles went too slowly—I was so anxious to get home again to Jim. The restaurant was supposed to have closed at nine. We arrived at ten-thirty to find a scene neither of us could believe.

"Good Lord!" said Ed.

We looked at each other incredulously. Like members of a chorus, there were assembled on the sidewalk before the darkened restaurant half-a-dozen bus boys in starched cotton uniforms, eleven waitresses in matching starched cotton uniforms, five un-uniformed individuals who I guessed were customers of the restaurant, conversing with the big genial restaurant manager. John's bicycle was standing in front of the group, with a sleepy John sitting in a patrol car, struggling to carry on a social conversation with the policeman who sat beside him.

For almost ten hours I had been stewing inside, frantic with worry about things I wouldn't even admit to myself. Then after Ed had called that John was safe and unharmed, I had begun to grow angry with John. I was angry with him for betraying my trust, angry with him for putting his father in the embarrassing position of having to watch me play the man's role in going after his son. For thirty miles that anger had built up in me, an aftermath of all the frustrations of the past days, of the worry of this one, and finally, the relief. I don't know that I ever really wanted to murder anyone—but by that time, I wanted to beat John until I was just one stroke short of it. At that moment, there was nothing Christian in me, just an ugly savage resentment. It was just as well Ed and the chorus were there.

I got out of the car and put my clenched fists into my coat pockets. I was too angry to unclench them. I walked over to the patrol car and told the policeman we had come for John. John jerked his sleepy head toward me, not sure whether to smile or be serious. He looked very much pleased with himself, but he could tell I wasn't feeling friendly, so he put away his smile and scrambled out of the patrol car.

Meanwhile, Ed had gotten out on his side of the station wagon, and that was the first signal to action for the chorus. Genial Manager stepped forward and with a loud Genial Voice, approached Ed. "That's really a mighty fine boy you got there. I told that boy if he didn't like things at home, just to come back down here any time he wants and stay with me, and when I come through Princeton, I'm going to stop and see him. Yessiree, that's a mighty fine boy."

I didn't know what John had told them, but there was no doubt he had made it mighty convincing. There was no point in explaining, though Ed managed to make it plain he owned no part of the child, but was just the juvenile judge. I wished I could have detached myself as easily. One of the waitresses had stepped forward to help me, and evidently she was more perceptive than the rest, for she offered me a word of sympathy. "I guess you were awfully worried, weren't you? How long has he been gone?"

I answered bitterly, under cover of the "genial" conversation. "Since early morning. He took his book money; I know it is all spent, and his father is lying at home worrying about him, too sick to come, and John adding to his troubles. Then that ridiculous man telling John he approved of the whole thing!"

John crawled into the back of the station wagon and lay down. Ed lifted his bicycle in beside him. By the time we left, John was already asleep.

By morning, it was too late to punish John. Also, I feared I might be unreasonable if I did, for I was still very angry. I made myself talk quietly to him about the responsibilities we have toward each other in families, but I fear it went in one ear and out the other.

Finally we figured out that he had long been upset because he realized his father was dying. Unfortunately, we hadn't talked to the children about it, and John was worried about what would happen after his daddy died. In his own mind, going by what had happened to him before, when he was almost five, he decided I would place all three children for adoption again, because we wouldn't have a home of our own anymore. He could not bear the thought, and so would run away.

When we realized what was troubling him, I made an opportunity to talk with him about it. The anxious, eager way in which he responded struck my heart. It takes so little to reach the heart and mind of a child. So little effort, but I had not made even that. I had been so engrossed in Jim and his needs, trying so hard to spread myself thin and to keep up with the house and the church, and to appear to do it all normally, that I had been giving my children only superficial attention.

I assured John that, whatever happened, we would remain together, and once he knew that, he was satisfied. From then on, he felt free to bring up the subject again when he wanted to talk about it, instead of keeping his worries inside himself.

Marie, now four, told me more easily she was troubled. She walked to the store with me one day, holding my hand, talking as she went.

"Mother," she asked earnestly, "If people just stay sick, and stay sick and stay sick, they're going to die like Mrs. Craig, aren't they?"

"Well, darling, if they can't get well, perhaps it is better if they do, for they will go to Heaven and be with God. Sometimes people *do* get well, but sometimes they do not. We have to let God decide what is best for them."

"Oh." She said no more, apparently content with my answer. But from that day on, she separated herself from Jim, and did not want any of the men she knew to pick her up or to play with her. She transferred her attentions and affections to me, where she had always before very obviously preferred Jim. It was a strange method of self-protection, and Jim was quick to notice it—but being Jim, just as quick to understand.

"Children are funny, aren't they?" he said.

The fact that Jim was dying was not quite so readily apparent to Carol, now almost three and a half. But the fact that he was suffering was very clear to her. She watched me intently when I massaged his head and his feet; then when I went away, she would go to perform the same office, crooning gently, "Oh, Daddy, Daddy," as if she could lighten his sufferings by the sound of her loving voice. She petted him and hovered over him, wanting to make some return for all the love and joy he had given her.

The new educational building had gone slowly for so long: for months, it had seemed to be no more than a hole in the ground, with a steel skeleton hovering over it and a crew of sidewalk superintendents watching its progress. Finally, in September, construction was complete.

The new brick building made the old brick seem shabbier

than ever, so the congregation went the second mile and had
the church building cleaned and the old joints pointed up with
fresh mortar. The old and the new now seemed one harmoni-
ous whole. The enclosed court formed by the passageways between the old and new buildings had been only a raw, debris-
covered patch of clay when Jim had been hospitalized in June.
By October, Lois Ratliff had wrought a miracle, transforming
the hideous little court into a lovely formal garden. The dark
leaves of espaliered magnolias and laurel gleamed against
the brick walls, and ivy borders flanked a paved brick floor.
In the center of the court stood a fountain surrounded by
potted plants.

It looked settled, as if it had always been there, a gracious
and quiet spot for meditation on the wrought-iron benches, or
a charming place for a reception. When the doors on the street
and the court were open, it seemed to beckon passers-by. Once,
as I was leaving the church, a stranger came in. When he
saw me, he felt he had to explain: "It just looked so beautiful
in here, I had to come see what it was."

The new building was dedicated in October. When we went
home from the service, Jim said, "I'm glad I was able to see
it done. Now, if I could only see the bonds paid up in full.
I hate to leave a debt behind me, for a new minister ought to
be able to initiate his own projects, not be hampered with a
debt others have made before him."

But that was not to be.

As the months went by the humiliations of the flesh were ever
increasing. Jim's legs and ankles were more and more swollen.
His legs had to be bandaged each morning, unwrapped when
he rested after lunch, and bandaged again when he got up.
For many months he had been on a salt-free diet, in addition
to the usual diabetic restrictions. There were new shots, and
pills by the handful. Jim said little about his trials and tribu-
lations, but seemed ready enough to learn from them, to com-

pare his own trials with those of members of his congregation, and even to find material for his sermons.

One Sunday morning I read in the church bulletin the sermon topic, "The Order of the Juniper Tree." It seemed an odd title, and I was curious to know what Jim would do with it. The reading was from the First Book of Kings, and concerned the prophet Elijah.

In a day-long demonstration on Mt. Carmel, God had given Elijah a spectacular victory over the false prophets of Baal. When the people of Israel saw the power of God, they had fallen on their faces and said, "the Lord He is God." In this moment of victory, Elijah had said to them, "Take the prophets of Baal; let not one of them escape." They were taken, and Elijah slew them at the brook of Kishon. But when Jezebel heard how Elijah had slain her four hundred prophets, she sent a messenger to him, saying she would have his own life by the next day.

After reading from the Scriptures, Jim began his sermon:

Poor Elijah! Only the day before, he had seen God send fire and rain down from heaven, and in God's strength had conquered the prophets of Baal, but the next day Jezebel had only to send a message, and he was afraid. He rose and fled for his life, past Beersheba, a day's journey into the wilderness, sat himself down under a juniper tree, and he 'requested for himself that he might die.'

All of us have our days of victory, when things go well and according to plan—apparently both our plan and God's. Then we rejoice and feel strong, convinced we are truly God's Chosen Ones. But then there comes a day when things aren't going according to *our* plans, and we don't even stop to wonder if it might not still be according to God's plan.

Like Elijah, we just hear about trouble, and we don't even wait for it to come to us. Forgetting the power of God, we are afraid, and rise up and flee into the wilderness, find ourselves a juniper tree to hide under, and cry out, "Lord, this is too much for me to bear, let me die right now!" All of us have our days when we are self-appointed members of the "Order of the Juniper Tree," when we're tempted to flee from whatever problem or trial or perplexity is awaiting us. . . .

I knew Jim was not talking of generalities, but of himself.

Yet beyond his sermon on "The Order of the Juniper Tree," Jim made little mention of the awful regimen of medication, transfusions, and double diets which were his daily portion, and of the inner weariness and occasional despair which must have haunted him.

Cold weather came early that fall. Though he was weak, though the raw winds renewed the possibility of pneumonia, Jim did not spare himself. He saw a job to be done, people to be developed "in the nurture and admonition of the Lord," and the time was short.

There was a heart-wrenching courage in the way he went about it. He drove only when necessary—then slowly and with great care. Otherwise he walked, so he would not be dependent on me, and to maintain what little strength he had. Slowly he walked through the streets of Princeton, to and from the church, walked to make those calls that were near enough, his spirit triumphing over his slow lumbering gait.

In the oppressive cold, his face was lifted a little into the wind, and as he walked, he seemed to grow in stature. We were all a little awed by him. . . . Where did his strength come from? How could he go on? In his Homburg, his dark overcoat, and carrying the big umbrella that served as a cane and kept him from falling, he pushed himself on—his face lined with pain, his back stiff with determination. At times somehow, you could see in him the young man he had once been—bearing aloft the ideals of his youth. But when you looked again, there was only a tired man, old before his time, plodding heavily and painfully onward, up a flight of stairs, and knocking at a door —the shepherd, calling on his flock.

Perhaps the very best work of his ministry was done in these four months of fall and early winter. As pastor (and the word actually means *shepherd*), the minister is in a very real sense the representative of God. His spirit of compassionate Christian concern for his people is his mediation of the forgiving, redeeming love of God for man. By the very simple fact of being who and what he is, the pastor in his calling brings the support of God, and of the Christian fellowship to reinforce and uphold his parishioner. The unconscious response of the individual when he sees his pastor at his door is, *"Why you cared, you came to me—then God cares, He will be with me, too."*

The specific troubles of individuals I never knew, beyond what was common knowledge in the community, for Jim was scrupulously careful not to betray a confidence. But every congregation has a cross-section of all the problems which beset man: in every place are the troubled, lonely, fearful, guilty, perplexed, discouraged, and Jim was a man who inspired confidence.

Like many a wise and sensitive pastor, Jim had the ability to read much in the unguarded faces turned to his during formal worship, and where he saw trouble, or sensed some hidden need, he tried to make a pastoral call if the person did not come to him first. Shyness, uncertainty, or even the American trait of self-reliance often prevented people from coming even when they wanted help. Here, a call from a sympathetic pastor can open the door, and once the problem is stated, the resources of the church can be called upon to help in its solution.

Always, Jim's heart was in his pastoral work, but in these last months of calling, it took on even greater meaning for his people. For if he cared enough to come and to counsel in spite of his own pain and suffering, then his care had to be very great indeed—and his suffering was also a bond of fellowship, as it were, his sympathy with *their* suffering!

One day I was out on an errand when a man I had never seen before stopped me. He was gaunt and plain, wearing bibbed carpenter's overalls.

"You Preacher Huff's wife?" he asked.

"Yes, I am."

"I got to tell you what that man means to me. I never saw anyone like him before. He's a good man and he makes me wanta be good, too.

"I never saw a good man suffer so. Somehow, it don't seem right . . . but I'm glad I know him. . . ." His voice trailed off, as if surprised at the depth of emotion he had revealed. My heart went out to him for loving Jim and seeing God through him. From a man little used to words, this was a real offering.

What a very long way we had come in ten years of marriage! The years had gone swiftly, but had brought us so much. Since our first year, when I had been insistent that Jim keep telling me if he loved me, we had both grown tremendously in our ability to express love.

One night, as I worked at massaging away the pain and tension of his day, the utter ridiculousness of our situation hit me.

"Jim," I said as I began to laugh, "none of my fine young dreams of romance included massage!"

He laughed, too. "Baby, I'll bet they didn't. But you'll never know how wonderfully romantic it is to have someone who cares enough for me to do it!"

"Darling, it's the charm of your magnetic personality. I never loved you more."

Flippant as the words were, after I had said them I realized how true they were. I *had* never loved him more. We had begun our marriage with all the rapture and high hope of young love, and after the early agonizing adjustments, our first years of living together had been amply filled. Yet, the greatest fullness of love had come in service. In small, trivial, constant acts of devotion, love had had its greatest flowering.

This wonderful quality of love which permeated and overflowed our lives quickened the senses and added zest to the days in a time which would otherwise have been unbearable.

Of course, there were days when I was a full-fledged member of "The Order of the Juniper Tree," when I felt the world too dark, and my present burden a heavy one. These times did not last long—and never with Jim, for his spirit was unwavering, and there was always joy in his presence.

For eight weeks before Christmas, Jim taught a communicants' class for young people, and on Christmas Day received six of them into the membership of the church, our own John among them. The following Sunday, New Year's Day, he received one more child on profession of faith. It seemed to us a miracle that we could welcome the New Year together, and Jim had been able to preach every Sunday since his vacation in August. His indomitable will, together with ability to draw on the power of the Holy Spirit had again and again carried him through.

The first week in the New Year, Jim had urgent personal business in Nashville. We knew there was risk in taking the trip—but things had been going reasonably well and we felt it was a part of "setting his house in order" to manage his business affairs as well as possible. We drove down. The children had all—as had half the folks in Princeton—been smitten with violent intestinal flu the week before, but had recovered quickly, and we had left them at home with a nurse.

On the way home, I became as violently ill as the children had been, and was completely unable to drive.

"If you can climb over me," said Jim, "I'll drive us home. It's too cold to stop." He was right; it was well below freezing.

"If you know two bigger idiots than us, I don't want to meet them," I said. "You shouldn't be trying to drive."

"Baby, I'm not half as sick as you are at the moment."

I couldn't argue the point. I was miserable, though I knew it was nothing serious. We had been talking in a light vein, and not really meaning it. I went on, "Honey, we've been dragging this out so long, why don't we just die now and get it over with?"

He answered in the same light tone, "Can't do it baby."

"Why not?"

"Afraid of the dark, baby. Afraid of the dark."

At that, I suddenly sat up straight, shocked at his reply. He couldn't be, he just couldn't be afraid to die. "Jim," I exclaimed, "you don't really mean that, do you?"

He realized he had startled me, and he put out his hand to cover mine. "No, Jane," he said quietly. "I certainly *don't* mean it. . . . Oh, I can't see any reason to go on living with a body like this—but I hate to leave you alone, to bear all the responsibility of the children, though heaven knows you've had most of it for a long time now. No, Jane, I'm not afraid to die. Like Paul, I believe 'for me to die is gain' and I'd like to go, for it seems there is so little left I can do. Yet I know there is something, or I wouldn't be left. As my body has gotten heavier and harder to handle, I've prayed I might die— but Jane, it seems so selfish to want to take the journey and leave you behind. Besides, I know you'd miss my good company. . . ."

The last sentence was said lightly, and he patted my hand. "Oh Jim, oh Jim, I love you . . ." I couldn't say any more, for conflicting emotions welled up within me. Laughter and tears, love and sorrow.

That was all he said about dying. He had faced it, had accepted it, and yet he would not run before the Lord to meet it. He would take each day as it came, and use it as best he could.

Jim got us home safely, then he came down with the same bug. I was quickly over mine but Jim was already so weak that he went into pneumonia again, and was bedridden for weeks, with penicillin and the usual routine of extra transfusions and medication. Another round lost—but the merciful end was not yet. There was still a long journey to go.

In February it was cold and rainy. It took Jim two weeks to get over his pneumonia. I was determined not to let him go out any sooner than I could help, so I volunteered my own services instead of his for those of his chores that I could perform. One of these was a weekly prayer meeting he had been conducting, using the lives of the apostles as the theme. The first night I took his place, he had planned to talk on John.

I had always liked John's gospel and found his message of God's love heart-warming, but before I began to prepare for this meeting, I had never been especially aware of the man or his history. John had been born in a well-to-do family and was used to social position. His mother wanted the best of everything for him, and had done her bit to try to secure it for him and his brother James (even to asking Jesus to save them special places in Heaven). John was ardent and impetuous: when the people of a little Samaritan village had not believed as he did, he had wanted to call down the wrath of God on them, and had stormed away, shaking the dust of the village from his feet. Jesus reproved him, and James with him—but he affectionately named them Boanerges, or "Sons of Thunder," for their fiery spirit.

But through the years John's spirit was tempered and refined, until it emerged in the remarkable gospel of love which bears his name. The *Interpreter's Bible* added a description of John's doctrine of the ministry: "The true pastor is he who, hearing the voice of Christ and accepting his authority from Him, receives eternal life himself and is able to feed the flock in green pastures and to lead the sheep beside still waters."

That last sentence was so like Jim. As I sat back to digest what I had read, it suddenly occurred to me that Jim Huff's story much resembled that of the "beloved disciple." His youthful impetuousness and impatience with those who did not believe as he did, his healthy enjoyment of his wealth and social position (which probably had kept him from the ministry in his early years), his growing zeal for the Lord's work as a layman, and finally his full commitment and acceptance of God's will all had their parallels in the life of the apostle. So completely had he accepted God's authority that his cup overflowed, and enabled him in his ministry, even in his terrible illness, to "feed his flock" on God's love.

One morning, just after Jim's recovery from pneumonia, he called me as soon as he woke. "Jane," he asked, "come look at my eye. Is there something in it? I can't see."

My heart sank. I looked carefully into his eye, but could find nothing visibly wrong, "Well honey," Jim said resignedly, "I guess you'd better phone Ralph."

When Ralph had seen Jim, he explained that there had been a large hemorrhage in the back of the eye. "All we can do is keep you quiet and hope the blood will be reabsorbed—if it is, you will see again, if it isn't, your vision will remain just as it is now. If you'll feel better about it, though, you might go down to the Vanderbilt Eye Clinic to see if they can suggest anything."

We were content with Ralph's diagnosis—yet, once Vanderbilt had been suggested, we felt we had to consider it. After all sight is a very precious thing, and if anything could be done. . . . Of course, we ended by going.

In a way, it was only time and strength and money wasted, for neither nature nor medicine could restore the vision in that eye. That was gone, but at least we had done what we could. We assumed life would be somewhat more complicated than before, but much the same. Jim could no longer read, but he could see enough to get about, and he didn't need eyes to preach. For the study required, I could be his eyes. At least he could stay active, I thought.

But as we left the hospital, the doctor explained that, to preserve the sight of the other eye, Jim must stay in bed for the next three months. I can remember the anguish with which I heard those words. Three months in bed? Why, he could never get up again after that, and if it were a choice between sight and activity, I'd have chosen activity. But I kept silent. We acquiesced to expert opinion.

There were two things I learned in this period when Jim was confined to bed. For one thing, I gained further insight into the problem of suffering and its meaning in the lives of men. For another, I realized just how wonderfully buoyant the spirit of a man can be in spite of adversity. Despite all the hardships now imposed upon Jim, he weathered it so cheerfully that he carried me and the children with him.

At first I was rebellious. I almost wanted to shout at God to either leave Jim alone or let him die, that I couldn't bear to go on watching him beaten down, blow by blow. But then, I had always known Christianity was no magic charm to ward off evil or suffering. Christ himself suffered and said, "If any man will come after me, let him deny himself daily and take up his cross and follow me."

I had long since learned God is ready to use suffering to the enrichment of our souls if we will let Him, and I had begun to think it possible that Jim's Christian witness would not be complete without it. His time of suffering gave him the opportunity for living entirely on faith. As long as he had every blessing: talent, health, and riches, he was a good man, but *only* a good man. But when these were gone— when he had stood fast through every trial, then he proved himself truly God's man, and the love of God carried him triumphantly through every need.

I also learned that trials come not entire, but minute by minute. I found we could always get through one more minute. I couldn't have understood these things earlier in my life, but God has His own way to prepare us for the experiences we are to meet. All the years of the little services in the church, the little experiences in prayer and faith now gave me strength and faith for each day. Like the manna of old, there was just enough for each day, yet that was as much as I needed. I learned that God indeed gives "Power to the faint; and to them that have no might He increaseth strength."

Jim had always read and studied so much, it must have been dreadful to have to depend only on me and on his radio for the mental stimulation he so enjoyed. I think he feared it might be selfish to depend on me, and it bothered him if I missed any of my normal activities. I would gladly have skipped them all, but because he cared I went. Each Sunday night I went to my Junior High Christian Endeavor, to church and club meetings—but only if I thought Jim knew about them. I preferred not to let Jim hear of invitations—unfortunately the phone was right by his bed, and there was little he did not hear! Because I continued to go out, I continued to receive invitations. I "forgot" many things, particularly when I found myself reading to Jim something he found especially interesting.

In spite of everything, we had a wonderful time together during this period of forced inactivity. How I looked forward each day to the time when I could go into Jim's darkened room to read to him. There was so much to say, so much to learn. These months of reading opened new doors to me. I had thought myself fairly well read—now I realized how little I knew. I would read blithely at top speed and trip past an unfamiliar word. Sometimes I would guess right, and keep on reading; other times, Jim would explode with laughter.

"Jane," he would shout, "What did you say?"

I would try to repair the damage, but my second attempt might be as bad as my first. It gave him such innocent amusement to catch me in a mistake that I never minded. Often I felt assertive enough to get out the dictionary to argue with him—but he was almost invariably right.

After two months of enforced rest, even Jim's patience could no longer hold out. He decided that no matter what happened to his sight, if he was ever to get out of bed again he'd better do it now. His health and spirit seemed to take a turn for the better, and in the flush of false optimism we decided to take a short vacation and visit my sister Martha in Florida in March. We rationalized our decision with the hope that the warmth and sunshine would do Jim good.

Although we were both tired from the drive, our first day in Florida seemed very pleasant. But Florida weather changes with dizzying speed. By late afternoon, it had begun to turn cold, the skies clouded over, and Jim began to seem abnormally sleepy. By night there was a penetrating dampness. We slept badly, and Jim was hard to rouse in the morning. At first I attributed this to fatigue and a poor night's sleep, but as the morning progressed, he remained groggy. His face was puffy, and his eyes were swollen half shut. I couldn't get him fully awake, and suspected that he might be going into a coma. I needed a doctor right away but didn't know any in Orlando, where we were staying. I had seen a Presbyterian church close by, so I walked over to ask for help.

With characteristic Christian charity the associate minister, Mr. Bowers, located a doctor at once. Unfortunately the doctor's office was full of patients so he could not come to Jim. Mr. Bowers drew me a map to show me how to get to the office, across town about a block from the hospital.

I went back to my sister's and tried to rouse Jim enough to get him to the car. "Baby, let me sleep," Jim complained. "I don't want to go to the doctor."

He was so tired and so sick. *"Why should he go?"* I thought. *"Why should he be bothered again? Why couldn't we let him be, let him sleep, and be bothered no more?"* But you have to do all you can, you have to make every effort, so I patted his shoulder and spoke sharply to wake him.

"Jim, get up," I said. "You've got to see a doctor. If you won't get up, I'll have to send for an ambulance."

He stirred faintly. "Oh, Jane, please leave me alone," he pleaded. "Please let me sleep."

"Jim," I said desperately, "come on! You know I have to take you."

With difficulty he opened his eyes and looked straight at me. "Yes," he said slowly, "yes, I guess you do."

I pulled at his awkward and heavy body to help him, first into a sitting position, then up on his feet. Martha took one side and I took the other. He put his arms over our shoulders and did his best to help as we half-dragged and half-pulled him out to the car. It made me ashamed to be a party to his humiliation, but there was no choice.

I opened the windows as we drove, and the sharp air helped to rouse him, so that I was able to get him into the doctor's office without help. The nurse was waiting for us, lead us straight to an examining room and the doctor came at once.

One look was enough for him. "Let's get some of the information we need," he said, "and get you right over to the hospital."

Jim spent the remainder of his "vacation" in the hospital. It was both heartening and depressing to see how much temporary help intensive medical treatment could give him. After these hospital stays, when Jim was given special medication and many blood transfusions, he grew stronger for some time. He generally reached a plateau where he remained for some time, until things inevitably began to go wrong again.

Jim was released from the hospital the day before we were to leave for Kentucky. When I got him into the car, he said, "Don't go straight to Martha's. Take me for a drive, and let me see *something* before we leave."

I turned north from the hospital and drove slowly through Orlando. In thirty minutes leisurely driving we reached the little town of Winter Park. Both of us agreed it was the loveliest place we had ever seen, a quiet, inviting community of wandering, tree-lined streets, spotted with many small lakes. It was a lift to our spirits to admire the pastel houses and lovely gardens.

"If I could make any plans about living," Jim said, "this is where I'd like to come and settle down. It looks like a perfect place to raise children. When we make our fortune and retire," he added lightly, "we'll come back."

On our return to Kentucky, Jim was able to take up his work again. It was good to see him in the pulpit once more, and to see him able to get about, however slowly and painfully.

The first Sunday after his return, Jim ordained several newly elected officers of the church.

Among them, Carl Sparks was ordained as an elder, and Reg Lowery and Arliff Walker as deacons. Jim gave a sermon at the ordination service which contained a bit of wry humor out of his own experience.

Sometimes, when men are elected to offices in the church, we all rejoice that these particular men were chosen, for they seem, from among our number, to be the best suited for these jobs. I know, though, you have all occasionally seen a man elected as elder or deacon and wondered why on earth *that* man was chosen. You can count off on your fingers half a dozen or more of his known sins or failings, and you wonder how God could possibly want or use a man like him.

Some years ago I was elected an elder by my congregation back in Rockwood. My daddy shook his head over it, and said, "That's one time the lower element in this church got the upper hand . . ." He was probably right.

I'm sure there were those in the congregation who questioned the wisdom of letting such a frivolous person as myself serve as an elder. But because I had been elected, I was ordained and consecrated with a laying on of hands by those who had been ordained before me. At times I may have been a good elder; at other times I *know* I was a poor one. Eventually though, that ordination led me to the full evaluation of my gifts and responsibilities and brought me into this pulpit. . . .

You see, I don't believe the lower element *ever* gets the upper hand when men are called to serve in the church. It is my conviction that when a congregation elects a man to office, they are led of God; it is God himself, directing His people, who calls men forth, who calls men to leave behind them all that was worthless in their lives, to strive toward that which is worthwhile—to put off the old man and to put on the new nature of godliness.

Some men answer the call in full service, some only in part, while some take only the outward office. I believe that God has called each of the men we ordain today. Let us each pray with them and for them, until they are lifted out of themselves, unto the life to which God has called them, until they change us, and our church and our community.

In the pulpit Jim had shown some of his old life and strength. It was short lived. By the time he got home, he looked dreadfully tired. Each respite was so brief and was followed by such pain and weariness that it seemed they had been bought too dearly.

Now Jim seemed to realize he couldn't go on much longer. One afternoon, when the session was to meet at the house, Jim told me, "Jane, I thought for a few days I was going to have strength enough to do something this time, but I'm so tired just from preaching I'm afraid I don't have enough left to give the church."

"What are you going to do?"

"I'll tell them just how I feel—tell them I'd like to have another three months, to see whether I have any useful service remaining to me. By then the decision ought to be clear cut, to go or to stay."

Carl Sparks sought me out privately after the meeting. "Jane," he confided, "from the way Jim talked, we felt there won't really *be* any decision by the end of three months. Of course we want to do what will make Jim happy and give him peace of mind. Many of us have thought that even if he resigns, you all ought to stay right here in the manse as long as you want to."

I was deeply touched. "How nice of you, Carl!" I said. "But if Jim does live until June, he'll want to move on and leave the manse free for a new minister."

Suddenly, Jim's strength failed so greatly that there was no question of his getting out of bed. The change was so sudden and drastic, it was shocking to see. It was a relief, too, I must admit, for we had been expecting it for so long. His life and strength seemed to ebb even as you looked at him. He became so weak it was impossible for him to eat, almost impossible for him to drink.

Ralph came each morning and night to do what he could. As he left one evening, I asked if Jim would die. No doctor likes to be put on that spot, but he did answer, "Well, he certainly can't live long like this."

When I went back into Jim's room, I saw Jim knew it, too. I was reconciled. I believed he wanted to die in Princeton, and was satisfied it was to be so. As if we had spoken of it aloud he called me. "Come here, Jane."

I went to his bed and knelt down beside him. He took my face in his big gentle hands, and looked at it as if he would memorize it. "It's been good, baby. Did I thank you for taking such good care of me? It's been so much more than I deserved." He could shape the words only with difficulty.

"Oh, God, don't let me break down and cry here. I'd never stop." I struggled for a light answer. "Don't be foolish. You've always traveled first class, so you might as well be ushered out in the very finest style."

"Yes, baby, right into my golden chariot," he finished facetiously. I kissed him, and the dangerous moment was past.

The fact that Jim could still laugh in the face of death made my tasks seem easier.

Yet, I knew Jim was in dreadful agony, and still he did not die. I knew he wanted to—I knew he felt he had done all he could do. It was difficult to watch him, a torment to be able to do nothing to relieve or alleviate his pain even for a few minutes.

Ralph was as upset as I. He finally arranged a three-way telephone hookup with Jim's two doctor brothers-in-law, White

Patten in Chattanooga and Sanford Monroe in Pine Bluff, and these three doctors decided on a very drastic course. It involved enormous transfusions of serum albumin and repeated injection of a most appalling drug, which coursed through his body like a raging fire. Ralph tried through our local Red Cross to obtain serum albumin—but without result. Now, many long distance calls to Louisville and Washington brought thirty-four vials of the precious stuff, to be given intravenously twice a day so long as it—or Jim—should last.

"This would be easier to do at the hospital," said Ralph, "but I know Jim would rather not go. Can you manage?"

I could. We stripped the room and borrowed from the hospital what equipment I didn't already own. This was the very worst time we had to endure, for the treatment was even more fearful than the illness. It was absolutely all I could do each morning and evening to nerve myself to go through the ordeal again, to stand by and help while Ralph began it, then to take over after he left. It was torture.

The worst of it was that apparently it did no good. Still we went on with it. The only thing that got me through was that Jim could still be funny about it. True, his was a grim sort of humor, but his contagious gallantry kept me going.

Once, when he was in such agony that he rolled and tossed on the bed, I unthinkingly remonstrated, "Jim, you've got to be quiet until this is done."

He shouted back at me, "Woman, could you lie quiet if you'd been stung by a whole hive of bees? Why can't you let a man die in peace? This is hell before I even get through the gates, and I had some hope of going to a better place!"

One day, he surprised me by saying suddenly, with no preamble, "Jane, if you cry at my funeral, I will sit up in my coffin."

I was so startled that the quick tears almost came to my eyes. Somehow, I blinked them back and laughed at him. "Yes, Jim, I know you would."

Usually, though he was passive and inert, exhausted by the ordeal, and continued to lose strength until I didn't see how he could live.

As usual, the generosity of our friends knew no bounds. Betsy Morgan took in the children, and the ladies of the church quietly arranged among themselves that someone should stay in the house with me all the time.

There was an isolation to the house, as if we had gone off by ourselves and left everyone else behind, except for the ladies who came in the morning to keep their companionable vigil.

George Eldred came by to tell me everyone was so concerned about Jim they were having another special prayer meeting on his behalf.

Bernice told me about it later. "People just left everything, Jane," she said, "and came. I was supposed to give an organ lesson, but I cancelled it. Everyone else apparently just left whatever they were supposed to be doing and came to pray. Mayme Curry left her classroom, and came down to lead the service. She spoke to us before the prayers, and said this could be a time of testing for our church. . . ."

Then there came a turning point, and Jim began to mend—I felt that we, like Jacob of old, had been "wrestling with the Lord." I did not know whether it was prayer or medicine which pulled Jim back from death into life once more, or whether it was for Jim or for ourselves we achieved the blessing.

I had not wanted Jim to pull through this crisis just to face another. If he couldn't be *well,* it would be better for him to be dead than to suffer endlessly. Yet, we had all pulled at him: praying for him, doctoring him, dragging him back from the border beyond which there is no return.

I was troubled about it until Ralph Cash said, "We have to do all we can, all we know to do. When we pull him back like this, we have to just hope he can hang on until somebody dreams up something which might really restore him to a semblance of health. There is so much in medicine we are just on the threshold of discovering—we can only hope some of these discoveries will be made in time to save Jim for a life of usefulness."

And in the long run, the seemingly useless medical experiments might lead to fullness of life for someone else, even if not for Jim. Science must prolong life as it can, each time hoping someone, somewhere, will come up with a better answer.

That was the humanist answer. But it was another answer that finally gave me peace: I had been troubled because after all the prayers, Jim was partly restored—but not enough for any real usefulness. It suddenly came to me, *"God just doesn't operate that way."* Prayer does indeed release power—but it is *power according to His will,* and God doesn't do things halfway. The key, I think, lay in the thought I had had once before: in some way, this suffering completed Jim's witness.

During this time of trial, Jim's sisters descended upon us like ministering angels. First Claire came, then Betty, and later, Anne. As Jim began to regain strength, the children were able to come home, and with Bet to help, we were able to manage a household which at least seemed normal, though Jim was still undergoing his very strenuous treatment. At least he was becoming a bit inured to it, and did not have such violent reactions to it.

With Jim much stronger, and summer nearly with us, I was faced with another difficult decision. John clearly needed another operation on his eyes. When I helped him with his studying, he invariably read a word to the right and below any word at which I pointed. With such a handicap, I wondered how the child could read at all. Once again, I thought it would be better for him to have surgery before Jim died rather than immediately after. Jim agreed, and, more important, so did Bet.

I knew it would make Bet more than nervous going through treatments with Jim twice a day, but she didn't turn a hair.

"I'll be glad to, Jane," she said. "The girls won't be any trouble, and Jim. . . ."

"Yes, I know," I finished it for her. "You love him enough to sweat it out with him, and I love you for it."

As we drove to Nashville, John said bravely, "Well, Mom, at least I'll be able to swim as soon as school is out by getting it done this month instead of next."

So, with the help of Jim's sisters, we got through those two ordeals. Jim continued to mend slowly, and John's operation was a complete success. By June, however, Jim knew there was no longer any possibility of his being able to preach further. We resolved to leave Princeton quickly.

Jim asked me to call the session to meet at the house. He told them it was clear he could serve no longer, and was resigning as of the first of July. He said he intended to preach the last Sunday remaining in his term, and asked that he be allowed to make his own announcement from the pulpit, if the session had no objection. They might have been dubious—he was so terribly weak—but no objection was voiced.

When the day came, the church was full.

Who could know what it cost Jim to part with his people? To know that for him there would be no other church, less than three years in the ministry, when he had hoped to have twenty. . . .

From his expression, no one could mark this day as different from any other. As he came into the pulpit, the lines seemed to drop from his face, and he lost himself, as always, in the job he had to do.

The choir sang the call to worship. Jim delivered the invocation, then led the congregation in the Lord's Prayer.

Then when the moment came for announcements, he said quietly, "As some of you know, I asked the session to meet with me to give them my resignation. I asked that they take the proper steps to have Presbytery dissolve my relationship with this church. As soon as that is done, you will need to set

up a committee to begin searching for a new pastor. The session has asked me to announce a congregational meeting immediately following the service two weeks from today. Dr.
Mack will be asked to preach that morning and act as moderator for the meeting.

"Mrs. Huff and I will be moving within two weeks. We want
to thank each of you for the love you have shown us—the help
and forbearance you have given during this past year. We
are very grateful to you. You can be sure our love and prayers
will remain with you as you seek a new minister, and as you
continue to work together. It is my hope you will receive your
new minister as graciously as you have received us, that you
may together find God's loving spirit."

The words and the manner seemed almost commonplace,
and might have been, but for the great love he had for them,
and they for him. The quiet moment was charged with drama.

Then, quietly as always, he began to preach. I remember no
word of that sermon—and I doubt if anyone else does. But if
we do not remember the words, I think all of us who were
there will always remember the man and his message. His first
sermon in that pulpit had been "God's Man," and he stood
before us, two and one-half years later, having proved himself
to be "God's Man," "strong and of good courage," through
every trial.

After the sermon, Jim raised his hands in the familiar sign
of benediction. As we bowed our heads, he put his heart into
the familiar words of blessing: "May the Lord bless you and
keep you, may the Lord make His face to shine upon you, and
give you peace, now and forever. Amen."

Bernice began to play, the choir sang the "Sevenfold Amen,"
and Jim Huff walked from the pulpit to return no more.

We wanted to leave Princeton as quickly and as cleanly as
possible, and it was up to me to find a new home for us. Jim
wanted me to find a place where the children and I could live

permanently after his death. My first thought was Rockwood, yet I dreaded returning there. We had been so happy in our years there that I couldn't face making a new home in a place full of old associations. Yet I felt Jim would want to return to the land and people he knew best, so I prepared to make the best of it.

As usual, Jim sensed my dilemma, and took the burden from me. One day he looked at me suddenly and asked, "Baby, do you want to go to Rockwood?"

"No, Jim, I honestly don't. Do you?"

"No, you can't ever really go back. I just thought you'd have more help in taking care of me if we did go. But I'd like to have our own things around me—you always make such a pretty house. . . . Why don't you fly to Florida and see if you can find a house in Winter Park?"

Winter Park had appealed to me strongly during our brief visit to Florida in March, and my reaction was enthusiastic.

I flew to Florida, and spent a fruitless day house hunting. When evening came, I was terribly discouraged. I had seen nothing within our means that we could live in permanently. I went to bed most disheartened.

But at eight o'clock the next morning, one of the real estate agents called me. "You know, I've had a house on my list for a long time. It doesn't sound like what we thought you might need, but it's a pleasant place, with a secluded little garden. Something tells me you ought to look at it."

I met him there half an hour later. The house was deceptively small looking, set back from the street, and built in a U-shape. I saw at once that it needed glass doors at the base of the U, and a floor-level terrace to connect both wings, where Jim could sit and enjoy the garden. I knew also I had found my house. I asked the agent to leave me there for a while to think it over carefully. An hour later I called Jim. He was delighted and told me to go ahead.

I made an offer, and in a matter of hours, we were home-owners once more. I caught the next plane back and was in Princeton before midnight.

Jim told me that while I was in Florida, the four members of the family who ran our local gas station had dressed in their Sunday best to call on him. They told him they hated to see us leave the community, because we had meant so much to everyone. Jim said it was especially touching, for they were people for whom a formal call was unusual. They were not members of our church; so far as I know, their only contact with us had been as we drove in and out of the station—yet Jim had won them all.

We could not get over the way people came to us to express their appreciation for what we had done in Princeton. But *we* had done so little; it was God who had done so much.

Jim wanted to leave at once to cut short emotion-draining farewells. I was pushed to get the packing done, and it was done in just three days. All our friends came to help. A number of high school boys worked heroically to lift and carry. I tried to keep Jim's room quiet, but it really wasn't possible. The noise and confusion were very wearing on him, but he did not complain. When the movers came, and it was time to take his bed apart and put it in the moving van, I took Jim down to a neighbor's and he went to sleep. It was very late before I was able to go down to pick him up. I helped him down the steps and into the car. We paused to pray we might harm no living creature on our journey, and I turned the car southward.

As I drove out of town, we both felt a terrible sense of finality. Jim laid his big hand on the seat between us, and I laid mine on his. "It was a mighty good two and a half years," he said, "in spite of my troubles." He began to speak of the individual members of the church, who had helped us, of those to whom we had grown close. We spoke of our work, of the little we had seen accomplished and all that remained to be done. For us, whatever the opportunities, they were gone; whatever the work, it was done.

You can never tear up your home by the roots without strain, but this was the hardest move I ever made. The trip was long and wearing, and despite what seemed careful planning, the new house was left a cluttered chaos by the movers. Worst of all I sorely missed the loving ministrations of all the friendly people in Princeton. Here I knew no one, and felt very much a stranger and alone.

Fortunately Jim's generous sisters had sent John off to camp, and our two girls, as usual, were well behaved as angels and quiet as mice. My main worry was Jim.

The long drive to Florida had a bad effect on him. By the third day, I knew he had to have a doctor immediately. The local Presbyterian minister, Oswald Delgado, suggested Dr. Hurst. When I called, he came at once, even though it was the Fourth of July.

He gave Jim a brief but thorough examination. "Look," he said, "let's put him in the hospital for observation. That's the only way I can get a true picture, and the only way I can tell whether or not I can help him."

I was a little surprised to hear myself say, "Let's *not* put him in the hospital. He doesn't like hospitals, and you can't learn a thing we don't already know." I sketched a brief history of the events of the last twenty months. "Jim knows what's happening to him," I went on, "and he's content. But I'm almost at the breaking point. In addition to Jim, I have children to care for and this house to settle. I want to be with Jim, to read to him and make life while it lasts as pleasant as I possibly can for him. I can't do it if you cart him off to a hospital. . . ."

Poor man. I must have been slightly hysterical by the time I finished. He gave me a sharp look. "You *do* have your hands full," he said. "And I guess maybe you're right. We can do al-

most as much for him at home as we could in the hospital."
He did a good deal, and Jim was much more comfortable by
the next morning.

Months before, when Jim's eyes had failed him so badly, I
had taken over the management of our finances. For the first
time, I realized how great a portion of our income he had
put into insurance. In the past two years we had sold all of
our securities and had borrowed a good deal of money, but
when Jim died, I would be well provided for.

I blushed with embarrassment. Early in our marriage, I
had criticized Jim for his use of money, for giving so far beyond the tithe, for his extravagances (so many of which were
really for others). I saw that if he had managed all these things
and all our living expenses, plus this huge program of insurance, he had been more than wise. How exactly like Jim to let
me criticize and never say a word in his own defense! I was
almost angry with him for letting me think poorly of him.

As I struggled to do the many extra tasks of straightening
the house, I grew very tired. One day Jim looked apologetically at me and said, "Baby, I wish I had been a little more
careful of money."

"No, Jim," I said vehemently, "I wouldn't have changed
any of it. It took me too long to understand fully what you
were doing, but now I know. It's been so wonderful to live
with you, to see someone who loves others more than himself.
Even if you did love yourself well," I teased, "you spread so
much joy along the way! Never dare apologize to me again!"

By October Jim had only strength enough to struggle out
of bed once or twice a day, and could stay up for only a few
minutes at a time. In two years of varying degrees of practical
nursing, I had picked up most of the skills necessary to the job.

Once, as I finished bathing Jim and was starting out with
the bathwater, he said, "Jane, you must marry again after I
am dead."

I stopped where I was. Suddenly I could see nothing in

front of me. "Must marry again." I stood very still and thought it over. Yes, we had said that, long ago at Skylot. I must not stay alone for the rest of my life. But *now,* to talk of it now? I could not bear it. I couldn't talk about it.

I struggled for composure and tried to avoid a serious answer, holding the washbasin in numb, unfeeling hands. "And who would be wanting to marry me," I said with false lightness, "a tired, worn-out woman with three children to be raising."

For once, Jim wasn't amused, he answered fiercely. "Any man would be more than lucky to get you."

It sounded as if he were straining to get out the words. I couldn't look to see. If I had turned, and seen on his face the compassion and love and pity which must have been written there—I would have fallen across the bed, and buried my face on his shoulder, and cried, and cried, until I could have found an end to grief, until the touch of him, the strength that still remained to him could have strengthened me and given me solace.

But when he already had so much to bear, so much pain in his grotesque and difficult body, I could not add to his burden. I could not ask him to comfort me again as he had for every trivial hurt through the years. For the greatest sorrow, my help and comfort would have to come from the Lord —I could not ask more of Jim.

I kept my face turned away from him as I went out the door, saying in as normal a voice as I could manage, "I'll see, love. I'll look around and see if I can find one to suit me—though it took so long to catch the last one, I doubt I'll ever manage the feat again." And then I fled, to cry alone.

Jim never stopped teaching me, advising me—training me, as it were, for the time I would be alone. Once, I recall his counsel caused me to break my promise to myself that he should not see me cry. I thought I was hurt by someone's thoughtlessness and selfishness. When I expressed my outraged feelings in full to Jim, and was flouncing out, he called me back. "Jane, come here," he said mildly, "I have something to tell you."

I sat on the edge of his bed. "What is it?"

"Don't be angry with me for showing you—but I have so little time left, and you must learn some things about yourself." He paused for a moment as if he hated to go on. "I wish you could have seen a mirror a few minutes ago. You would know what I mean. You were wearing your pride way out in front. Your face was pinched and ugly. You should never look like that—and you shouldn't think thoughts that make you look that way."

I knew he was right. I had been angry, even bitter. I didn't realize it would show so badly. It is not easy to look at your faults—but I knew he was right. "Oh, Jim," I said wearily, "sometimes I wonder if there is any hope for me. I get so discouraged with myself." The admission cost me too much, and tears began pouring down my face.

"Oh, Jane," he said in despair, "I didn't want to make you cry. You are a beautiful woman in so many ways. You must remember that you have been so many beautiful and lovely things to me, and I would do anything I could to spare you hurt or pain. But I can't be with you much longer. You've got to see where you are vulnerable, learn to see people as they are, and not to expect more of them than they are capable of giving.

"You and I have lived in the rich-giving warmth of Christian love," he went on, "and our love for each other has been a kind of insulation for both of us. You've stood between me and the hurts of the world, you've often stood between me and my own mistakes, and I've tried to do the same for you. But now you'll have to begin again, and you'll often be with people who are not Christian, who cannot look at others with that abundance of love—and *you* are going to have to do all the giving."

By now, I was sobbing unashamedly. "Oh, Jim, every time I think I have learned something about living, every time I think I have achieved a little stature, I see how far I still have to go, how little I have yet learned. And some of the lessons are so painful."

"Yes, but without them, you wouldn't have become the person you are. You were lovely at twenty, when I first saw you—lovely with the idealism and the beauty of youth. But, darling, I love you far more at thirty-six. You must keep your mind and your heart open all the days of your life so you will go on growing in love."

Jim's sympathy and understanding had loosed the flood-gates. It had been over a year since Earl Caldwell's simple mention of "Come Before Winter" had unexpectedly reduced me to tears. Now that winter had come and gone. I thought how very much it had brought to us. How great a measure of love and compassion had been shown to us on almost every hand, and how rich our life together had been through this year.

There had been many blessings, and there was still much to be thankful for. But there was also much to cry about. I could not control my sobbing, and Jim reached up to pull me down beside him. "Here, Jane, put your head down on my shoulder. There, baby, there now."

And he comforted me as he had when I was only a bride—when I had cried over some petty thing I cannot even remember today. If he had understood me then, he surely knew what was in my mind now, and he held me close to him, giving from what little store of strength he had left.

At last my tears were exhausted. "Mr. Huff," I said apologetically, "I'm afraid you've had far more than your share of tears."

"Well," he said, "I guess it's just the lot of any man who takes a wife unto himself. You and I have had more than enough to laugh about, too."

We had been blessed with a mild and beautiful fall but in late October, several dreary days were climaxed by a turbulent, wind-lashing storm, ripping branches from the trees and flinging moss and leaves down upon us. With the windows closed against the storm, Jim's room seemed to grow small and oppressive. The rain beating against the windowpanes, the violent motion of the storm-tossed oaks outside gave a feeling both of depression and violence.

The violence reflected my own inmost thoughts: Jim was in pain, and I was discouraged and tired, and the violence outside brought to life a violence within me. It tore at me to watch Jim "bearing all things in patience and humility," with no word of impatience for all that was required of him.

"How long must this go on," I thought bitterly. *"How much longer must it last?"*

The next morning dawned fair and clear and I felt purified and refreshed. The world had a new, washed feeling. When I was reading aloud to Jim he suddenly began to cough violently. I realized he was hemorrhaging.

When I reached the doctor, he said, "We'd better get him into the hospital. I'll phone for the ambulance."

I phoned my sister Martha in Orlando who said she would leave at once to take care of the children. By the time I had packed a bag for Jim, Martha and the ambulance were both at the house. Two men efficiently moved Jim from his bed onto a wheeled stretcher and took him out into the brilliant sunlight.

"Well, Jim, at least you picked a beautiful day to take a trip," I said, with as much cheerfulness as I could muster. "Glad you didn't choose to make this journey yesterday."

The air was as sweet and joyous as on a May morning, though the debris from yesterday's storm, broken limbs, tangled moss, and piled leaves lay about us like the wreckage of dead hopes. As the stretcher was lifted into the ambulance, Jim said, "Yes, I think it was very clever of me."

It seemed that all the hospital scenes and all the transfusions were blended into one bad movie, drawn out too long. *"Please, God, let him go,"* I thought. *"He wants it so. Let it be swift and easy this time."* I was so tired of the long vigil, and of the heavy weight of knowledge of what I was losing; better to have it done, better to see it finished.

For three days Jim's strength ebbed lower and lower, but he never entirely lost consciousness. He would wake and sleep, and drift in a dreamy state between waking and sleeping, and life seemed to ebb downward with the gentle motion of a leaf whirling gently down from a tree, to settle to earth at last. There was an empty bed in the hospital room, and I stayed beside him night and day, never sleeping, only half dozing on the other bed when he seemed to be asleep, instantly awake when he needed me.

We had said all there was to say. We had spoken all the words of love. The only thing left to do was to sit beside his bed, so he would know I loved him with a steadfast love; to be there whenever his eyes opened, so he would know he could count on me; and to do for him every small errand I could think of.

As Jim's strength ebbed, so did mine. In the two full years since that "cold" which was really pneumonia, I had more than "walked the second mile." I had walked in faith, upheld by prayer, through all the time of testing. Now I realized I was very, very tired indeed.

Friday morning I left the hospital to go home and take a bath. I felt unspeakably grimy and dirty, and the hot shower was luxury. I dared not linger long, though, so I finished quickly, dressed in clean clothing, and hurried back to the hospital.

When I walked back into Jim's room his appearance was completely changed. He had fresh color, and his head was propped up a little on the pillow. He looked as if he had been given new life in the forty-five minutes I had been gone.

"Well, baby," he said with sudden strength and vigor, "it looks as though you're stuck with me still!"

"What has happened?" I said in amazement.

"I don't know," he replied. "Everything was drifting away, and I was content to be leaving, when suddenly I just seemed to wake up, and here I am."

Through the afternoon he continued to gain strength. By evening, it was more than clear Jim had pulled through. Now we were both anxious to get him home. When Dr. Hurst came in, he said, "I see you've cheated Death's bright angel again."

"Sure have," said Jim cheerfully. "This has been harder on Jane than it's been on me. She has no one to keep the children now, and she can't be in two places at once, so I'd like to get back home."

"Not quite so fast," said the doctor. "I think you're going to need two more transfusions. Then let's give Jane a chance to go to church on Sunday, and have the ambulance deliver you home after lunch. That will give her a little bit of a rest."

It was good to have Jim home again. It was good to have this crisis over, but I felt more tired than I ever had in my life. Once again I entered into my argument with myself about the sometimes dubious blessings of modern medicine. To what avail to drag Jim back just so far, when he was so ready to die? I had steeled myself so often to accept my loss, only to have the burden of care returned to me. It was such a confusing, contradictory feeling, and made me feel guilty that I could put it into such terms, because I truly loved Jim with all my heart, and was glad to do everything for him, even wishing I could do more. Nowadays, though, my thoughts and feelings seemed ever more confused.

It seemed to me that we had proved all the promises of God: "He giveth power to the faint, and to them that have no might he increaseth strength. . . . But they that wait upon the Lord shall renew their strength; they shall mount up with wings as eagles; they shall run, and not be weary; and they shall walk, and not faint."

Despite long habit in prayer, I could not properly pray. I just told Him what was going through my head; querulously, pitifully; *"God, I am tired."*

There are some things you should never say, even to yourself. Or if you say them, you should say them in prayer, asking for help to meet the temptation even as you recognize it. All I had to do was to "wait upon the Lord" to renew my strength again. But I did not do it. With queer inertia, all I could say was: *"God, I am tired."*

Then, like Peter walking on the water, when my faith failed, I sank. Faith had been the substance and strength for the multitude of my daily tasks, and it had been more than sufficient for my need. But when I questioned it—when I asked, "Why, Oh, Lord?" and "How much longer, Lord?"—I too, slipped into the waters.

I didn't just give up, fold my hands and quit—nothing so honest as that. But my spirit had set the stage, and my body took its orders. Next morning I was up as usual, fed the children, got them off to school, fed and bathed Jim, and turned to the house as soon as the last child got out the front door.

Then the flesh revolted. It seemed literally years since I had had an unbroken night's sleep. Ahead of me stretched more of the same: bandages to change, bedpans to carry, beds to make, books to read aloud, hurts to kiss well, and hurts I must only watch since no love could ever heal them.

I hadn't been honest enough with myself to realize I had begrudged any of it—but my body knew how to get out of it all. The room tilted, spun crazily, and refused to right itself. My stomach rebelled at this unnatural state of affairs, and I was thoroughly, violently sick.

There now. No one could doubt I was sick. I was disgusted with myself, but I had lost control. Too weak and dizzy to move, I lay on the floor, my face on the cool, refreshing tiles.

Finally, I was able to get as far as Carol's bed, but every movement only sent my world spinning once more. I lay there until noon, when Marie and Carol came home from kindergarten.

They brought me the phone book and pencil and paper, and I wrote Martha's number in large figures. Marie went away to phone. She was only five, and had had no experience in dialing, so she had no luck. She would report a busy signal, or nothing at all, and once she came back to say she had gotten the fire department.

I had not been in to see Jim in three hours, and I was terribly concerned about him, but I could not get myself off the bed. I gave Marie the numbers of two friends, Vivian Morris, and Delia Delgado, our minister's wife. At last, she got Delia.

"Mama said will you come give my daddy some lunch," Marie said sweetly over the phone, not giving Delia any inkling who Mama or Daddy were. Delia finally managed to get it out of her, and came at once with Vivian.

They fixed lunch for Jim and the girls, called the doctor for me, and called Jim's sister Betty to come from Tennessee to look after us all. They arranged for a night nurse to come, and sent a maid to come to the house next day to do the housework and look after Jim.

Bet arrived and in her easy way took over. Her first task was to see the doctor and get him to put me in the hospital. We all knew I would not rest at home, so I made no protest. While Bet was here I might as well get rested enough to carry on.

For four days I slept, waking only when someone came with food. The doctor made sure I was troubled by nothing more than fatigue. There was nothing else. I slept and slept and slept, listening for no one, knowing Bet was with Jim, and that he and the three children were well cared for.

At home, meanwhile, all the blood Jim had received in the hospital had done its rejuvenating work, and he became daily

stronger. For many months, he had not even been willing to
sign his name to legal documents—now he began to write letters to all he loved: old friends, parishioners, fellow ministers.
Everyone he thought of he added to a long list. These were
cheerful letters, laughing at his "incapacity," showing interest
in their concerns, and wishing God's blessing on each. He
wrote more than a hundred of these while I was in the hospital.
One to Orville Pearson who had just been called to the church
in Princeton. Orville later sent it to me, after he had read it
aloud to the congregation:

Dear Orville:

I do not know whether you have felt any sense of being held up
(is that the expression?) by prayer since you accepted the call to
the church at Princeton, but day and night as I have thought of
those lovely folk there, the way they treated me, the things we
together did, and even more we did not do, the more I lift you
all to God, supplicating His blessings upon you and your leadership
for them.

I am afraid as my only "flock" they will always seem to me to
be particularly mine. They were wonderfully kind people, and I
know you will find them as anxious to work with you as you are
to work with them. I am not enough of a judge of humanity to
make any suggestions to you as to how to work with any of them,
nor would I want to. My purpose in writing is to let you know we
will be praying for the indwelling of God's Spirit with you, and
to tell you how pleased we are you have gone on to Princeton.

God bless you all!

Sincerely,
Your Brother in Christ,
James A. Huff

In the hospital, my few days of sleep restored me, then I
began to read part of each day. It was fun to read to myself
again. I had loved the sharing with Jim through all the months
—but it *was* a pleasure to read swiftly once more, skimming
the pages, losing myself in the effortless flow of words.

I turned most naturally to Paul's epistles. I had once thought Paul mighty heavy reading, and it had once seemed to me that a Christian needed little more than the gospels. Now I knew Paul understood trouble, and his words could be a great comfort.

All things are for your sakes, that the abundant grace might through the thanksgiving of many redound to the glory of God. For which cause we faint not; but though our outward man perish, yet the inward man is renewed day by day. For our light affliction, which is but for a moment, worketh for us a far more exceeding and eternal weight of glory. . . .

"For our light affliction . . ." Had it really been any more than that? There was nothing I had yet had to face alone—I had Jim's confident laughing spirit with me every step of the way. I had been thanked for every effort and loved in return for all my love. If it seemed long to me, what is two years in God's sight? What did it matter how long? Was it for me to judge?

Jim's keen mind could see this as an opportunity for service. He had a willing spirit. Who was I to wish away the time, to try to cut short his witness—had he not given his life to *whatever* thing the Lord called him? I was ashamed of myself.

"Jane, don't always be running before the Lord," I could just hear Jim saying.

In Philippians I read, "I want you to know, brethren, that what has happened to me has really served to advance the gospel." (R.S.V.) Even as I had railed at God for making it last so long, I had known this was so. But it was comforting to read it again, to hold this verse to my heart and take new courage from it.

I was ready to go home, but the doctor would not dismiss me from the hospital. One more day—one more day, he said, until I wouldn't put up with it any more. Bet was to take the little girls to Tennessee for a visit, and brought them to the

hospital to tell me goodbye. When I walked out to the lobby
to see them, I was surprised to find I was exceedingly weak.
But it was a joy to see them eager and happy about the journey.

John was with Jim, a night nurse was to come each night
for ten more days, thanks to Bet's generosity, and the doctor
promised to release me from the hospital next day.

Jim looked wonderful. He had continued to lose weight
after coming home from the hospital, and was able to get
around the house once more, to his great delight.

I looked at him, and told him I should have left him long
since, he was so much improved. He chuckled and said Bet
had taken good care of him. But he made it plain he was glad
to have me home again.

We had settled down far from most of those who loved us,
yet they poured out their hearts to us in letters. One we received from the pastor, elders, and deacons of the Presbyterian
church in Rockwood. As I read it over to Jim, we could see
these men gathered in a group, talking it over, deliberating the
words to use.

I read the formal phrasing aloud:

We express our gratitude for the devoted service given by you to
your home church. Your witness and your deep spirituality were
an inspiration to all. . . . The work you did among the youth of
this vicinity is still remembered with praise by people both far
and near . . . We express the pride of this church in your wider
service to the people to whom you felt called to minister as pastor. . . . Your devotion and your faithfulness have spoken silently
to us of a deeply committed life and have challenged us to a deeper
commitment. We give thanks to Almighty God for the wonderful
way it has pleased Him to bless and use you to bring honor to
His Holy Name.

Submitted in the Master's Name. (and it was followed by two
rows of signatures.)

My voice caught as I finished reading, and Jim was as
moved as I. It was a thoughtful gift of love from these men.

I again felt ashamed—perhaps Jim had lived this long "that the abundant grace might through the thanksgiving of many redound to the glory of God."

The last night the nurse was with us, after she had bathed Jim, she came to me. "Mrs. Huff," she said, "I do not like the look of that leg. I think you had better call the doctor."

The doctor came and frowned over it, but made no explanation. He suggested a special preparation for bathing the injured area. It was several days before I learned what had happened: the circulation of blood in the area had stopped, and the awful incurable rot of gangrene was setting in.

At the time, I only knew Jim was in more pain than he had ever been. By morning it seemed almost unendurable. He was literally writhing in torment, and clammy perspiration dampened his forehead as he struggled against the pain.

I was in the kitchen when I thought I heard Jim shouting, and I ran back to the bedroom. To my astonishment, he was singing. I had been sure I would never hear his voice lifted in song again. Yet there he lay, his hands clenched, his body set and straining against the agony, his eyes looking out the window, where the sun shone, the sky was clear and blue, and the squirrels ran chattering from one tree to another.

He was singing "In the Garden":

> I come to the garden alone,
>   While the dew is still on the roses,
> And the voice I hear, falling on my ear,
>   The Son of God discloses,
>
> And He walks with me,
>   And He talks with me,
> And He tells me I am his own....

I was still holding a dish towel, and because I could not bear to look at him, I began to dust the dresser top, and, swallowing the awful lump in my throat, added my poor soprano to his full baritone. He sang the hymn through, then began "He Lives":

I serve a ris'n Savior,
    He's in the world today,
I know that He is living,
    Whatever men may say,
I see His hand of mercy,
    I hear His voice of cheer,
And just the time I need Him,
    He's always near.

What absolute conviction could bring forth such words at such a time! If I turned my back, it sounded no different from the hundreds of other times he had sung in joy and health, with just that sure conviction. Unshed tears scalded my eyeballs, and I sang with him until I could stand it no more, and walked out of the room followed by the sound of his voice.

Later that day, he said, as if it were torn from him, "I have prayed all day that this cup might be taken from me, 'yet not my will but Thine. . . .'" That single sentence was his only spoken protest against the agony.

My heart was torn and aching as I watched Jim suffer. Some things we finite mortals cannot understand, except through experience. As a mother, I had learned that my children often had to learn in this way—and however much it might hurt me to do so, I must stand aside and let my children learn through hurt or pain. God, the wise Father, must allow us to be hurt in order to let us experience the fullness of His love. I am steadfastly convinced that suffering does not come to us *without* some reason in God's plan.

Jim was always so far ahead of me in this respect—he had so long ago committed all his life to God, that perhaps this experience was designed for *my* growth. Jim could lie in agony and sing praise to God, so fully had he accepted God's will. Oh, if I could only learn such honest patience, if I could stop *planning,* planning, every bit of my life, and rest in God's will!

The pain became so intense that Jim could not bear the slightest touch on his body. No longer could careful massage work its healing magic: there was no surcease from pain. Our world narrowed down to this one room, this one spot. Continually I prayed he would be released, if it were God's will, and that He would strengthen us both if there were still more to endure. Consciously and determinedly I yielded myself to God's will. Then peace came again. When I stopped trying to make God do what *I* wanted, when I accepted this as being within His purpose, I was filled again with an indescribable sense of His love.

There are for some of us only a few times when we truly feel the presence of God. Most of us wander along through the desert of life, and most of life's experiences are the mirages of the desert, not reality, while those few times when God is very near are the "living water." Perhaps because our lives are so much filled with this world we are not really searching for the "living water," and are too often content with our mirages.

But when strength is gone and we can no longer rely on ourselves, then like weary children, we simply give up—and at once find God, who has been there all the time, if only our eyes had been open.

Looking back, and trying to describe it, words fail me. I only know God touched me then, and life will never be the same.

Jim grew steadily weaker, and found it harder and harder to eat. On Wednesday I fixed him a special supper, with a soft custard, bland and rich with eggs, for his dessert. I was not always successful with them, but this was smooth and good.

Jim ate it with pleasure. "You are so good to me," he said. "God knows how much I love you!"

Jim's suffering was so great that I took Dr. Hurst aside that evening and asked him to leave something to help Jim sleep, though Jim had always before refused sedatives. The doctor left two vials of Demerol, telling me to give one at a time by hypodermic, and to use the second only if the first did not work. Jim took the first without protest, but it made no difference at all. He did not even grow drowsy. About midnight, I gave him another, but this had no more effect than the first.

About two, Jim insisted that I get some rest, promising to call me if I could do anything for him. I was more than reluctant to leave him, but knew I could not go too long without sleep. I lay down in the next room and must have slept, yet I seemed to be conscious of Jim all through the night. I was up by first light.

Jim had not slept at all. His face was drawn with suffering. Truly he had been through the "crucible of affliction," and only the essence of the man was left. Yet he bore his pain patiently and even looked at me with compassion as I brought him his breakfast and began to feed him.

"Did you get any rest, Jane?"

"Enough, darling."

It was the fifteenth of November, and there was just a hint of crispness in the air, like a bright September day farther north. Beyond the terrace the poinsettias were a magnificent blaze of color, in brilliant contrast to the clear blue sky. Curiously, my mood was one of elation and anticipation, as if some lovely thing were to happen that day. After too little sleep, one tends to feel rather than to think, and I worked swiftly, the curious mood of elation still upon me. As I worked, the words of "The Holy City" came to me as Jim had so often sung them. In my heart I could hear him singing it with all the old power and joy.

I went to check on him and found him asleep for the first time in more than forty-eight hours. "Oh, thank you, God," I breathed, so relieved to see him at peace. His arm was in an awkward position. I moved it so he would not awaken cramped, then went about the house, doing the odd jobs which had accumulated over the past few weeks.

My elation persisted, and so did the words of "The Holy City:"

Last night I lay asleeping,
  There came a dream so fair,
I stood in old Jerusalem,
  Beside the temple there;
I heard the children singing,
  And ever as they sang,
Methought the voice of angels
  From heaven in answer rang.

As I worked, the chorus came to me, full and clear:

Jerusalem, Jerusalem,
Lift up your gates and sing:
Hosanna in the highest,
Hosanna to your King!

Jim was deep in sleep when I looked at him again. He
looked more at peace than he had been in a long, long time,
and I wished with all my being that he might never wake,
might never know pain again. *"Go, my darling,"* my spirit
went out to his, fervently willing him away. *"Go, love, go and
be free."*

There was upon me such an urgency that I could not be
still. I was in no mood for thinking, and I left the room to
find something to do with my hands. I swept each room in
the house, dusting and straightening behind me. The peace of
cleanliness and order spread through my little house, and to
my heart Jim's voice still sang:

And then methought my dream was changed,
  The streets no longer rang,
Hushed were the glad hosannas
  The little children sang;
The sun grew dark with mystery,
  The morn was cold and chill,
As the shadow of a cross arose
  Upon a lonely hill

As the shadow of a cross arose
Upon a lonely hill.

When I looked in again, Jim's color had changed; his breathing became heavy and labored. This was no longer sleep, but coma. I went to call the doctor. And still that song flowed about me:

Jerusalem, Jerusalem,
Hark how the angels sing:
Hosanna in the highest,
Hosanna to your King!

"I'll come at once," Dr. Hurst said.

"No," I said. "Unless there is something that should be done, I don't want you to come. I just wanted to be sure I have done everything I should do," I explained.

"You've done it all," was his quiet answer.

I was glad he had nothing more to suggest. I was tired of last-minute remedies. There comes a time when a man should be allowed the simple dignity of death.

Jim would not have wanted me to sit by his bed, so I did not, but moved in and out, doing what little useless things I could think of. The words of the third verse of "The Holy City" eluded me, so I went to the piano and picked it out:

And once again the scene was changed,
New earth there seemed to be,
I saw the Holy City,
Beside the tideless sea,
The light of God was on its streets;
The gates were open wide,
And all who would might enter,
And no one was denied.

The last chorus was a flood of sound, mightier and more triumphant than I had ever heard it:

Jerusalem, Jerusalem!
Sing for the night is o'er!
Hosanna in the highest,
Hosanna for evermore.
Hosanna in the highest—
Hosanna for evermore!

As we see it from this side, death is cold and gray, but death for a Christian is no lonely thing at all. Some splendor hovered here. I stood by the bed, watching Jim's labored breathing. A strong man relinquishes life slowly.

I had lost track of time. John surprised me when he came in from school. "Oh, Mother," he whispered, "why does Daddy make that funny noise?"

I guided him out of the room, making a sign to him to be quiet. I do not like dissembling, but John knew all there was to know, and I saw no point in adding to his burden. "Daddy's asleep, son, and I guess he's having a hard time catching his breath." I tried to divert his mind. "How was school today?"

"Oh, okay. Mom, may I go fishing? I've got some new hooks."

"All right, son, but please just go down to the foot of our street so I can find you if I want you." I was relieved that he had something to do.

I returned to Jim's room. There was now nothing of *him* left in this frame still struggling for breath, with a heart still beating after its occupant was gone. Here was left only a shadowy semblance of life holding on by some frail strand to the life that had been. Then, even as I watched, it drew one breath deeper than the rest, and breathed no more.

I put my hand on that cold wrist. There was no pulse. *"Ah, love, thank God, you are altogether free."*

"Hosanna, Hosanna in the highest. . . ." The music was with me still.

I knew Jim had heard the music, too. As all his life had been set to music, I had no doubt he too heard music through all of this day. The words may have been different, and the tune lovelier than any I heard, but I am sure there was music for him who had taught so many others to sing.

The death of a Christian can be lovely and triumphant, and Jim's had been just that. His earthly life was over. It was complete and perfect. His own voice had sung the requiem. Now he was lifted up into a new life.

"Oh, my love it was wonderful. It was rich beyond measure, and blessed in remarkable ways. Thank you."

And I turned away and went to the telephone.

I called Jim's brother, Woods, first. "Oh, no," he said incredulously, as if Jim's magic charm and love of life could not die, despite all the suffering which had gone before.

I called the doctor, then the Delgados. Delia answered, and I told her Jim was dead. Oswald was not there, and she promised to try to find him, saying he would come as soon as he heard.

"Are you alone?" she asked.

"Yes."

"But you ought not to be alone," she said. I told her I did not mind. Of course I did not mind being alone. I had tended this body so long—what difference did it make that Jim was gone and only his body remained? Because she could not drive, Delia let the matter go, a little reluctantly. "I'll call Oswald," she said.

Dr. Hurst came and made his perfunctory check. He asked how he could help me. Even when the undertaker came to take away Jim's body, he was still uncertain about leaving me alone.

"Thank you so much," I assured him. "But you don't have to stay."

"But you ought not to be alone."

"I don't mind being alone. I have been ready for this for a long time, and anyway, you know I'm not really alone. God is with me."

My worldly friend looked very doubtful and concerned.

"Oh, go on," I said. "I know how full your day is, how many more calls you probably still have to make. Really, I'm perfectly all right."

Reluctantly, he went on.

I went into the house, and at that moment John came again. There is no gentle way of breaking the news.

"John, darling, you know Daddy has suffered so long. Now he is dead and will not have to suffer any more."

Poor John. In the back of his mind he had thought that now we three were together again, things might go differently. "Oh, no, Mama," he cried, "not Daddy." But then he straightened up—he knew, and he accepted the news.

I was still so full of the music of "The Holy City" that I sat down at the piano and played and sang it through, and John sat and sang it with me.

Then my sister Martha came, and friends, and Oswald Delgado.

As our minister, Oswald had long since talked to Jim and me about Jim's approaching death. He knew we were both ready for it, so was little to say now. All he could do was to show his deep sympathy and concern.

"Jane, do you have enough money? Do you need anything? Jim told me that in time you would be provided for, but that you might have a difficult time at first." I had in my purse just fourteen cents, but that day's mail had brought two money orders which would be sufficient for our fare to Rockwood and other immediate needs.

"If I had seen you this morning, Oswald, I would have had to ask for help—but I have enough now, thank you."

The next night I was in Rockwood. Woods and Louise and others of the family had waited up for me. Louise's house was shining and lovely. We chatted only a few minutes, made plans for the next day, and I went up to bed. It had been fifteen years since I had first visited Rockwood, and had first walked up those same stairs. What a lot of living had filled the years between!

I remembered Jim's long-ago wish that his funeral could be a party. Of course, I couldn't make it a party—but I knew I would not cry. Jim had a hymn he used with groups of children which put my feelings into words:

> Jesus took my burden
> I could no longer bear
> Jesus took my burden
> In answer to my prayer...
> And left me with a song.

Truly, my heart was singing. How could life with Jim have left me any other way? I had been blessed beyond all measure in sharing his life for eleven years. I had no illusions about the grief which would come later. I knew I had lost my way of life, my way of love. But I had also learned we lived only *today*. I had strength to do all that remained to be done.

My task at the moment was to greet all those who came— to share with them my own sense of the triumph of Jim's spirit. I still had that sense of exaltation which I had the day Jim died, so it was easy to share my feeling with others. It filled my heart to see how many came to the house to be with us all.

Jim's body was to arrive on the afternoon train. The day was almost tranquil, warm in the sunlight, but cool in the shadows. We sat in the car a few minutes, but I was restless and got out to walk around.

When we arrived, there had been no one at the station, but as we waited, others began to come. The train was late, and gradually the station yard filled with people. Most of them I knew. Some came over to speak, others just stood by waiting. It's a rare train that takes on or discharges more than two or three passengers in Rockwood, and I wondered idly who all these people had come to meet.

At last we heard the train in the distance, and the earth

picked up the vibration of the wheels. The engine clattered past us and came to a noisy halt. To my surprise, no one got on or off—just the porter and conductor, opening the baggage car. The waiting hearse moved up to take its load, and the men in the station yard took off their hats. I realized that this crowd had come in silent tribute to Jim. "Home is the sailor, home from the sea, and the hunter home from the hill."

In Florida when I had gathered up the clothes I was to take to the funeral home, I came across a little mustard seed that Jim had carried for many years. On impulse, I picked it up, and put it in the pocket where he had always carried it.

In Rockwood, when the undertaker opened the casket, he found it and returned it to me. I just dropped it into my own pocket, but when Woods asked if there was anything I wanted before the casket was closed, once more I put it in. Why? I wondered—but then someone came, and my attention was diverted.

It was weeks later that I began to think why. I lay in my bed on Christmas night, and the full grief of my loss washed over me. I had gotten this far with scarcely a tear—but I had planned only this far. I was bone-tired, yet put off going to bed, and even watched a boring program on television to put off the time. Then, when I stepped over to turn it off, Jim's face smiled at me from the family portrait on top of the television cabinet—and I began to cry. I could not seem to stop, until at last I thought of the mustard seed.

I remembered Jesus' parable of the mustard seed, one of the smallest of seeds, which a man took and sowed in his garden. It grew and became a tree, and the birds of the air made nests in its branches. We, who are so small in God's great world, give imperfectly of our little offering, and God, in his magnificence, takes that little offering and blesses it, until our lives, which were small, become rich and fruitful, and a shelter and a resting place and a comfort to others.

Yes, it was symbolic that the mustard seed should be

placed in the earth with Jim's body. God will give the increase to the seed of his witness.

Jim's body lay in state at the house overnight, and burial was planned for Sunday afternoon. The house was filled with flowers, and friends came and went. It was touching to see them and evidence of their thoughtfulness. They came from all of Rockwood, Old Town and Clymerville and Chestnut Hill; from Knoxville and Chattanooga, and on beyond. On Sunday came several cars full of friends from Princeton. They came from all walks of life, from all the periods of Jim's life. Children came, and their parents, grandparents, and great-grandparents.

If funerals serve any purpose other than to enrich under-takers, they are for the living, not the dead. If there is any comfort in them, it is in the gathering of friends and loved ones, and in the beauty of music and Scriptures. I had gone through the funeral service in the *Book of Common Worship,* and had chosen the most challenging and triumphant passages to be used in a very short service. I asked Ellen to play the most joyful hymns she could—and reminded her how often Jim had said he wanted the "Hallelujah Chorus" from the *Messiah* played at his funeral.

"I can't bear to do that one," she said, "but I'll make it as lovely as I can."

It was time to go. We all walked out into the afternoon sunlight slowly, so the family could assemble in some sort of order, and then moved on.

A minister friend came tearing down the hill just as we started across the street. He had barely time enough to get into the church before us. I couldn't help but grin as I caught his eye, and heard Jim's voice out of the past, "Preachers are always late."

The entrance to the church was banked with the flowers that overflowed the little church. We mounted the steps and went in, entering the familiar pews. We sat where I had always sat, where a thousand times I had looked up to catch Jim's eyes upon me as he sang the familiar hymns Ellen was now playing.

"Oh, my love!" my heart cried out as I looked perforce upon the closed casket and the masses of flowers before me. I was perilously close to tears—and Jim would have hated that. I could hear him say again, "Jane Huff, if you cry at my funeral, I'll sit up in my coffin!" And knowing Jim, I knew he would! Suddenly I was as close to laughter as I had been to tears.

The conviction that Jim's death was a victory came back to me again as the minister read:

I am the Resurrection, and the Life, saith the Lord: he that believeth in Me, though he were dead, yet shall he live: and whosoever liveth and believeth in Me shall never die. . . .

Meanwhile, at Princeton, the ladies were fixing flowers in the sanctuary for the installation of the new pastor, and others were in the kitchen, making last-minute preparations for the reception to be held in the fellowship hall after the service. Ministers and elders and friends from the Presbytery of Western Kentucky were driving toward Princeton, where many of them would learn for the first time of Jim's death.

Here, the formal words were said, the organ swelled out in joyous sound, and we followed the pallbearers out of the church, up to the beautiful wooded hill where we stood in the sunlight as the body was committed to earth.

Two hours later, in Princeton, the installation service for Mr. Pearson began. An ending and a beginning, and a continuity seen by God: As one pair of hands must drop the torch, another picks it up to carry the Light to all the world.